YA

WALLINGFORD PUBLIC LIBRARY
200 North Main Street
Wallingford, CT 06492

WITHDRAWN

AY

WITHDRAWN

WORLD HISTORY

THE RISE OF

ISIS

THE MODERN AGE OF TERRORISM

By Caroline Kennon

WALLINGFORD PUBLIC LIBRARY
200 North Main Street
WITHDRAWN
Wallingford, CT 06492

LUCENT
P R E S S

Published in 2017 by
Lucent Press, an Imprint of Greenhaven Publishing, LLC
353 3rd Avenue
Suite 255
New York, NY 10010

Copyright © 2017 Lucent Press, an Imprint of Greenhaven Publishing, LLC.

All rights reserved. No part of this book may be reproduced in any form without permission in writing from the publisher, except by a reviewer.

Designer: Seth Hughes
Editor: Siyavush Saidian

Library of Congress Cataloging-in-Publication Data

Names: Kennon, Caroline.
Title: The rise of Isis: the modern age of terrorism / Caroline Kennon.
Description: New York : Lucent Press, 2017. | Series: World history | Includes index.
Identifiers: ISBN 9781534560567 (library bound) | ISBN 9781534560574 (ebook)
Subjects: LCSH: IS (Organization)–Juvenile literature. | Terrorism–Religious aspects–Islam–Juvenile literature. | Terrorism–Middle East–Juvenile literature.
Classification: LCC HV6433.I722 K425 2017 | DDC 956.054–dc23

Printed in the United States of America

CPSIA compliance information: Batch #CW17KL: For further information contact Greenhaven Publishing LLC, New York, New York at 1-844-317-7404.

Please visit our website, www.greenhavenpublishing.com. For a free color catalog of all our high-quality books, call toll free 1-844-317-7404 or fax 1-844-317-7405.

contents

Foreword

History books are often filled with names and dates—words and numbers for students to memorize for a test and forget once they move on to another class. However, what history books should be filled with are great stories, because the history of our world is filled with great stories. Love, death, violence, heroism, and betrayal are not just themes found in novels and movie scripts. They are often the driving forces behind major historical events.

When told in a compelling way, fact is often far more interesting—and sometimes far more unbelievable— than fiction. World history is filled with more drama than the best television shows, and all of it really happened. As readers discover the incredible truth behind the triumphs and tragedies that have impacted the world since ancient times, they also come to understand that everything is connected. Historical events do not exist in a vacuum. The stories that shaped world history continue to shape the present and will undoubtedly shape the future.

The titles in this series aim to provide readers with a comprehensive understanding of pivotal events in world history. They are written with a focus on providing readers with multiple perspectives to help them develop an appreciation for the complexity of the study of history. There is no set lens through which history must be viewed, and these titles encourage readers to analyze different viewpoints to understand why a historical figure acted the way they did or why a contemporary scholar wrote what they did about a historical event. In this way, readers are able to sharpen their critical-thinking skills and apply those skills in their history classes. Readers are aided in this pursuit by formally documented quotations and annotated bibliographies, which encourage further research and debate.

Many of these quotations come from carefully selected primary sources, including diaries, public records, and contemporary research and writings. These valuable primary sources helps readers hear the voices of those who directly experienced historical events, as well as the voices of biographers and historians who provide a unique perspective on familiar topics. Their voices all help history come alive in a vibrant way.

As students read the titles in this series, they are provided with clear context in the form of maps, timelines, and informative text. These elements give them the basic facts they need to fully appreciate the high drama that is history.

The study of history is difficult at times—not because of all the information that needs to be memorized, but because of the challenging questions it asks us. How could something as horrible as the Holocaust happen? Why would religious leaders use torture during the Inquisition? Why does ISIS have so many followers? The information presented in each title gives readers the tools they need to confront these questions and participate in the debates they inspire.

As we pore over the stories of events and eras that changed the world, we come to understand a simple truth: No one can escape being a part of history. We are not bystanders; we are active participants in the stories that are being created now and will be written about in history books decades and even centuries from now. The titles in this series help readers gain a deeper appreciation for history and a stronger understanding of the connection between the stories of the past and the stories they are part of right now.

SETTING THE SCENE: A TIMELINE

Abu Musab al-Zarqawi establishes
al-Qaeda in Iraq (AQI).

ISI tries to absorb the
al-Qaeda–backed
militant group al-Nusra
Front, but al-Nusra
resists; Abu Bakr
al-Baghdadi establishes
the Islamic State of Iraq
and Syria (ISIS).

Al-Zarqawi is killed in a U.S. airstrike and Abu Ayyub al-Masri
takes his place as leader of AQI; Al-Masri announces the
creation of the Islamic State of Iraq (ISI) and declares
Abu Omar al-Baghdadi the commander of the faithful.

Abu Bakr al-Baghdadi
becomes leader of ISI
when al-Masri and
Abu Omar al-Baghdadi are
killed in an operation led by
the United States and Iraq.

2014 ·· **2015** ······················ **2016**

Al-Qaeda renounces ties to the Islamic State after months of fighting between al-Nusra and ISIS; ISIS takes control of Mosul, Iraq; Abu Bakr al-Baghdadi declares himself the caliph (ruler) of the world's 1.5 billion Muslims; ISIS renames itself the Islamic State.

U.S. officials say about 6,000 ISIS fighters have been killed; ISIS takes control of Ramadi, Iraq, the biggest city in the western part of the country; U.S. State Department declares ISIS to be a greater threat than al-Qaeda.

An ISIS car bomb explodes in a busy shopping area of Baghdad, killing at least 292 people and injuring more, making it the deadliest single attack in Iraq since 2003.

FROM ISLAM TO ISIS

In 2004, a man from the country of Jordan named Abu Musab al-Zarqawi, famous for the suicide bombings he coordinated, formed a group of Muslim fighters and named it al-Qaeda in Iraq (AQI). Today, this group is known by another name: the Islamic State in Iraq and Syria, or ISIS. President of the United States Barack Obama often referred to the group as ISIL (the Islamic State in Iraq and the Levant), and many simply call it the Islamic State. No matter what it is called, it is undeniably referred to often. ISIS has grown into a large Muslim extremist organization that has significantly—and negatively—affected the entire world.

What Is ISIS?

The main priority of ISIS is to spread sharia law worldwide. Sharia law is a system of morals and rules for Muslims to lead righteous lives, following the religion of Islam. Installing sharia law means that ISIS is trying to ultimately establish a global society that is similar to the ancient past of the Middle East. It wants to bring the whole world back to the seventh century—and it wants the whole world to practice the religion of Islam. In order to achieve this, ISIS's tactics often focus on terrorizing the parts of the world that practice different religions and hold different, and more optimistic, views on the future. ISIS is responsible for thousands of deaths. Between January 2014 and January 2016, 18,802 people were killed in ISIS-related violence in Iraq alone—not to mention the 36,245 people who were hurt or injured in some way. These deaths include hundreds of public executions, which are intended

The whole world is keeping a close eye on Syria, Iraq, and the surrounding areas.

to make a statement: Anyone who does not follow the rules of ISIS will face terrible consequences.

ISIS is a group that does not attempt to hide its horrible actions and intent—in fact, it makes an effort to publicly display its crimes. ISIS takes advantage of modern communication methods to promote itself and frighten its opponents. Social media platforms such as Twitter have become important tools for ISIS to show the world what they are doing. Through Twitter, it is able to show its enemies how powerful it is and recruit extremist Muslims in areas of the world far away from Iraq and Syria.

The destruction caused by ISIS is not limited to human life. Despite its commitment to Islam, ISIS has destroyed ancient Muslim holy sites in both Iraq and Syria. Its followers have been known to blow up holy shrines and mosques, as well as demolish valuable antiques, just to get a reaction out of their enemies. The antiques that are not destroyed are sold for a profit. This is one way ISIS makes its money. It also produces oil, taxes the inhabitants of its territory, blackmails and extorts citizens, and demands ransoms from foreign countries for the citizens its followers have kidnapped.

In 2014, ISIS controlled more than 34,000 square miles (88,000 sq km) in Syria and Iraq, which is an area a little smaller than the American state of Maine. In April 2015, however, it was estimated that ISIS had lost about a quarter of its land territory. The head of ISIS has claimed that he is Islam's caliph. This loss of land is especially important because ISIS cannot continue to claim that it is a caliphate if it does not own land or expand its territory.

ISIS is not invincible; past leaders, including Abu Musab al-Zarqawi, have been killed. As of 2016, the current leader of ISIS is a man named Abu Bakr al-Baghdadi. He currently lives in Syria because, according to Islamic prophecy, Syria is the country where the last battle on earth is supposed to take place. According to CNN National Security Analyst Peter Bergen, Dabiq, Syria "is where the Prophet [Muhammad, founder of Islam] is supposed to have predicted that the armies of Islam and 'Rome' would meet for the final battle that will precede the end of time and triumph of true Islam."[1] Those leading ISIS want to be on the front lines when that final battle begins. They are sure that their actions and beliefs will bring them straight to paradise after death, and anyone who is not an extremist Muslim will be defeated.

WHAT IT MEANS TO BE A CALIPH

The concept of a caliphate is very important to some Muslim people. It is how they have organized their religion since the death of the Prophet Muhammad. Muhammad is the most important figure in Islam, and he is regarded as the writer of the Koran, which is Islam's holy book. However, when he died, he left no one to continue his work. A caliph is someone who is recognized as an heir to Muhammad's leadership, and a caliphate is the area that he rules. ISIS's goal is to have this caliphate expand to cover the entire world.

What Is Islam?

In order to understand the Islamic State, it is important to understand the religion of Islam. The word Islam itself translates in English as submission or surrender. The religion has a lot in common with Christian and Jewish beliefs. It is monotheistic, which means it teaches Muslims to believe in only one God, whose name is Allah. Adam—the same Adam from the holy texts of Christianity and Judaism—is recognized as Islam's first prophet. Muslims believe that prophets are individuals sent by Allah himself to give the people laws to live by. Other prophets in Islam include Abraham, Noah, Jesus, and Muhammad. Muhammad is the central figure in Islam and is thought to have been the last prophet Allah sent to deliver his message.

It is also very important to remember that ISIS represents only a very small percentage of Muslims. Almost all Muslims say that violence in the name of Islam is not justified. A survey that was done in the United States in 2011 by Pew Research Center, which studies social issues and demographics, found that 86 percent of Muslims say that violence for the sake of their religion is rarely or never justified, while 7 percent say it is sometimes justified. Only 1 percent of Muslims in America say this violence done by extremists is justified.

Muhammad

The man who would become the Prophet Muhammad was born in the town of Mecca, in what is now Saudi Arabia, in the year 570. When he was only five or six, both of his parents died, so he lived with his paternal uncle.

Muhammad worked as a shepherd and helped his uncle with his merchant business. Older merchants nicknamed him *El-Amin*, which means the one you can trust. Around age 20, he married a distant and older cousin. They eventually had six children. Life was good for Muhammad, until he began to see Mecca as too prosperous. To Muhammad, wealth and luxury in the city were making it corrupt. He started going on long retreats to mountain caves outside of town to fast (not eat all day) and meditate. One day, he claimed that he was visited by a strong presence that gave him a message. After being visited by this presence several times, he shared what he heard with his close family. They believed that the words he recited were so beautiful that they could only have come from Allah. Eventually, these verses were written down and would

The Koran's name means "the recitation" in Arabic. This is a fitting title, because Muslims believe Muhammad recited the word of God to someone who wrote it down.

become the Koran (sometimes spelled Quran or Qur'an), Islam's sacred text.

Most people in Mecca, however, did not fully embrace Muhammad's claims, and they attacked him and his followers. There was even an attempt to assassinate him. In 622, Muhammad left Mecca for the town of Yathrib, and it was soon renamed Medina, which means the City of the Prophet. This is where the first real Muslim community was built. It quickly gathered more and more members. In 630, the Muslims had grown much stronger and marched

This piece of art shows Muhammad preaching. His face is covered, as it is in most artistic depictions of him.

to Mecca, being joined by many groups along the way. Even Mecca, which had rejected him so strongly eight years earlier, joined him without violence. Muhammad died in 632 and was buried in the mosque in Medina. Within 100 years, his teachings had spread as far as Morocco, France, and Spain.

Five Pillars

Islam is built on five "pillars." These are the five core ideas that define the teachings of Islam and Allah. The first is the *shahadah*, which is the most basic statement of faith that all Muslims believe in. It is generally translated as, "There is no god but Allah, and Muhammad is his messenger." The second is the *salat*, which is the daily ritual prayer of faith that must be performed five times a day. One component of the *salat* is that the prayer must be done facing the direction of the holy city of Mecca. The third is the *zakat*, which is a tax that Muslims must pay to the poor and less fortunate. The minimum amount is 2.5 percent of a believer's total wealth. The fourth is *sawm*, which is the fasting that must be done during the month of Ramadan. Ramadan is the ninth month of the Islamic calendar. It is the month in which Muhammad is thought to have received the first of the revelations of the Koran, which is 114 chapters long. Muslims cannot eat or drink during daylight hours during Ramadan. The fifth and final pillar is the *hajj*, which is the pilgrimage every Muslim must take once in their life if at all possible. The pilgrimage is to the most sacred place for Muslims: the shrine Kaaba in the holy city of Mecca, where Muhammad was born.

Along with the Koran, Muslims have a collection of traditions and sayings of Muhammad's, which is called the Hadith. These guidelines are what they aim to base their life and beliefs on. Frequently used, by both Muslims and Western media, is the word "jihad." Literally, this word means the struggle of an individual to follow Allah's commands, both at a personal and community level. It has been associated in modern times with radical Islam, and the word "jihadist" now refers to an Islamic militant. It is important to note that the original teachings of Islam do not encourage jihadist violence.

There are a number of different branches of Islam. The largest group is the Sunnis—they make up 85 percent of the world's 1.5 billion Muslims. ISIS is made up of Sunni Muslims. In the eyes of ISIS, some of their biggest enemies are Shia (also called Shiite) Muslims. The Shia make up about 10 percent of the world's Muslim population and run the Iraqi government. The biggest difference between these two groups is that the Sunni believe the first four caliphs after Muhammad's death were legitimate successors to Muhammad. The Shia, however, believe only the fourth caliph, Ali, and his descendants are the rightful successors to Muhammad, and they reject the first three caliphs. Although most Islamic violence happening in the Middle East revolves around these two denominations, there are also some additional smaller groups, including the Wahhabi, a Sunni sect in Saudi Arabia, and the Alawites, a Syrian Shia sect who observe some Christian holidays in addition to traditional Islamic ones.

The 1.5 billion Muslims in the world make up 23 percent of the entire planet's population, but only 1 percent of the adult population of the United States; 63 percent of the American Muslim population are immigrants. It is the second-largest religious population next to Christianity, and it is the fastest growing religion overall. It is projected to grow at a faster rate than the world's population as a whole. The Pew Research Center projects that by the year 2050, there will be 73 percent more Muslims than there are now. The number of American Muslims is expected have grown to 2.1 percent. This growth is expected because, on average, Muslims have more children than those belonging to other religious groups—Muslims average 3.1 children, while all other religions combined average 2.3 children. Muslims are also the youngest of all major religions; the average age for a Muslim in 2010 was 23, which is 7 years younger than the average age of all non-Muslims.

What Is Terrorism?

The media uses the words "terrorism" and "terrorist" so often that they have become synonymous with the Islamic

State. Unfortunately, many uninformed people have associated Muslims in general with the actions of a small number of extremists. In order to understand how ISIS wages its war against the rest of the world, it is necessary to understand what terrorism is and where it came from. The United States Department of Defense defines terrorism as using or threatening to use violence to intimidate other people or governments. ISIS is attempting to terrorize the Western world—meaning countries, such as the United States and much of Europe, that have roots in Roman civilization and Christianity—by killing and threatening in order to eventually achieve its goal of a global caliphate and sharia law.

Modern international terrorism is thought to have started in the late 1960s when Palestinians realized they could not fight the much larger Israel military. When Palestinians realized they would not win with traditional warfare, they started using urban terrorism. This means the radical Palestinians hijacked planes, kidnapped civilians, and bombed Israelis in a way that became a model for other small ethnic and religious movements.

In 1979, the Soviet Union invaded Afghanistan. This ignited a war that lasted until 1989 and sparked the creation of many terrorist groups. Afghanis could not take on Soviet Russia outright, but they could attack in very small numbers through bombs and kidnappings that would weaken the Soviets' will to fight. Volunteers from all over the Islamic world fought for Afghanistan. After the Soviets left that country in 1989, it had become a popular location to train terrorists. Because Afghanistan's Taliban leaders are sympathetic to terrorist causes, they have provided support, travel documentation, and training facilities for these extremist groups. The terrorist group al-Qaeda is the most famous group that benefitted from this environment.

Terrorism became coordinated and widespread with the creation of the Taliban, an Islamic political movement in Afghanistan. Since 1989, terrorist organizations have also attacked targets well outside of their geographic areas. In 1993, for example, there was a bombing at the World Trade Center in New York City that killed six people. The most famous international terror attack in history is the September 11, 2001, attack on the World Trade Center and Pentagon, which killed more than 3,000 people and injured 10,000.

Terrorism is directly responsible for thousands of deaths every year. In 2013, 17,958 people died in terrorist attacks around the world. More than 80 percent of those people were from Iraq, Afghanistan, Pakistan, Nigeria, or Syria. Of those 17,958 deaths, 6 of them took place in the United States.

CHAPTER ONE

BIN LADEN, AL-ZARQAWI, AND AQI

Although a vast majority of Muslims worldwide are peaceful believers, a small fraction of them, mainly located in Middle Eastern regions such as Syria and Iraq, have been spreading violence, fear, and hatred in the name of the religion as a whole. The United States and other countries have been fighting the rise of terrorism for more than 30 years, but it has been difficult to win significant victories. Many terror groups are structured so that there is a clear chain of command: If the leader is killed, one person can step up to fill their role. They do not fight in traditional formations or using common military practices. This makes it very difficult for members of anti-terror forces to fight them, because they have been mostly trained to fight other armies.

Terrorist groups, such as ISIS, do remain traditional in one important way—they need common soldiers. Because military action is constantly being taken against them, their soldiers are killed frequently. One of the greatest mysteries (and dangers) facing anti-terror forces is the widespread recruiting that ISIS has been able to accomplish. Extremist Muslims from all over the world have gathered to support the cause in the Middle East, and new soldiers join ISIS daily. One of the reasons they have been so successful in convincing others to join them is because of their history of leadership.

The Young Lion

The story of the rise of the Islamic State begins years ago in Saudi Arabia. In 1957, the seventh son of Muhammad bin Awad bin Laden was born in Saudi Arabia. His name was Osama bin Muhammad bin Awad bin Laden. The name Osama means young lion. Muhammad bin Laden was an immigrant to Saudi Arabia from Yemen and a self-made billionaire. He was the owner of a very successful construction company—so successful that it is credited with the restoration and extensions of the three most holy mosques in Islam: al-Aqsa, Mecca, and Medina. Years later, Osama bin Laden would proudly tell interviewers that his father sometimes prayed in all three holy places in one day. In the 1960s, Saudi Arabia's King Faisal had instructed his country that all construction projects had to be given to the bin Laden group.

Muhammad bin Laden was a polygamist, which means he was married to multiple women at the same time. This custom is legal in Saudi Arabia but illegal in many western countries, such as the United States. Osama's mother was the 11th of Muhammad's many wives. She was the only wife of Muhammad bin Laden who was not from Saudi Arabia; Muhammad had met her on vacation in Syria. Osama was her only child. People close to the family have said that the rest of the family called Osama's mother "the slave" and Osama "the slave child." It was highly unusual for rich and powerful Saudis to be born to two parents from outside the kingdom. The country of Saudi Arabia believes that family

history is important, and Osama must have felt like an outsider because neither of his parents could claim Saudi Arabian ancestry.

Outsider or not, Osama spent his childhood summers working on road construction; all of the bin Laden children had to work for the family company. In 1967, however, tragedy shook the family when Muhammad died in a plane crash. Osama was 10 years old. Although there were more than 50 bin Laden children, each sibling inherited millions of dollars. Their lives were similar to the lives of celebrities or royalty; the "slave child" had his own stable of horses when he was 15.

Interestingly, Osama was the only bin Laden child who never studied abroad. In fact, it is reported that he never even left the region of the Middle East. Many of his siblings traveled to Europe and the United States. Several of them were living in the U.S. on September 11, 2001, when Osama orchestrated major attacks on American soil that killed more than 3,000 people.

Osama bin Laden grew up as a dedicated Muslim, studying the religion in high school and college. Like most Saudis, he grew up around Wahhabism, which is a strict and anti-West branch of Islam. While earning his college degree, he became involved with the Muslim Brotherhood, a group of Islamic extremists who believed that most Muslims, including the leaders of Saudi Arabia, were not living according to the true meaning of the Koran.

Osama bin Laden, shown here, came from a very wealthy family and went on to create al-Qaeda.

Soviets in Afghanistan

Near the end of 1979, the Union of Soviet Socialist Republics, or Soviet Union (which eventually broke up, creating separate nations, including Russia), crossed the border into neighboring Afghanistan to establish control. The groups of anti-Soviet Afghanis were collectively named the mujahideen, or "those who do jihad," and they tried to prevent the Soviets from taking over their government. Mujahideen is now a term commonly used to refer to terrorists. Within two weeks of the 1979 invasion of Afghanistan, bin Laden went to Pakistan to meet some refugees.

After intense fighting, roughly 100,000 foreign soldiers had taken the major cities and populated areas of Afghanistan. Over the next nine years, the Soviet Union occupied Afghanistan while the mujahideen fighters, aided by bin Laden, tried to push them out. About 1 million civilians, 90,000 mujahideen rebels, 18,000 Afghani troops,

The Soviet Union bordered Afghanistan before it dissolved and a group of separate nations emerged.

and 14,500 Soviet soldiers were killed. This war paved the way for the birth of the Taliban in 1996 by leaving Afghanistan incredibly vulnerable.

Al-Qaeda's Origins

Although the Soviet Union eventually left Afghanistan, the damage was done. The country and the entire region had become unsettled; the environment was perfect for the emergence of terrorist groups. Al-Qaeda was actually created as a database for bin Laden. He wanted to compile as much information about his soldiers as possible so that he could contact their families if they died. It quickly expanded to be bin Laden's infamous group of anti-West extremists. For these recruits, bin Laden himself became a larger-than-life figure: a young man who had transformed from rich boy to warrior. However, intelligence sources say he only saw combat once—and very briefly. Regardless, his reputation was one of his most important assets. After all, a good reputation led to more recruits. Bin Laden eventually met Ayman al-Zawahiri, a surgeon who would become his right-hand man. In 1998, bin Laden and al-Zawahiri announced that their individual terrorist organizations—al-Qaeda and the Egyptian Islamic Jihad, respectively—would become a single organization.

Now presenting a powerful and dangerous front, their combined forces issued the following fatwa (religious decree): "The judgment to kill and fight Americans and their allies, whether civilians or military, is an obligation for every Muslim."[2] These radicals wanted to physically remove all presences that they deemed foreign and oppressive—specifically the Americans and Israelis. They hated the United States because it chose to back non-Islamic leaders in Israel and Egypt. To retaliate, al-Qaeda and other terrorist groups instructed their soldiers to cause as much damage as possible.

DID THE UNITED STATES HELP OSAMA BIN LADEN?

The Soviet Union and Afghanistan were not the only countries involved in this war. The United States helped Afghanistan fight the Soviets during the invasion by supplying weapons and money to the mujahideen, which means that the United States and Osama bin Laden were actually once on the same side of a fight. It could be argued that the U.S. helped bin Laden's extremist groups evolve by giving them weapons and money. Regardless, bin Laden claimed that he only tolerated the interference of the United States because they were providing what the jihadists needed.

Al-Zarqawi

Al-Qaeda's terrorism against the West reached far and wide among radical groups in the Middle East. In 1999, Abu Musab al-Zarqawi traveled to Afghanistan to ask al-Qaeda for money and recruits. He wanted to start an uprising throughout the Fertile Crescent, which is the land from the eastern Mediterranean to Iraq. Although al-Zarqawi was looking to bin Laden for funding, they had one major difference in beliefs. Al-Qaeda believed that all Muslims needed to band together to fight non-Muslims and the West. Al-Zarqawi, however, was preoccupied with establishing one group of Muslims that was more powerful than the other branches. Al-Zarqawi passionately disliked the Shia sect because he believed that they conspired with the West to persecute the Sunnis. As a result, he wanted to bring glory to the Sunni while destroying the Shia. Despite this difference, bin Laden decided to support al-Zarqawi because al-Qaeda had so few allies from Palestine and Jordan. However, bin Laden did not invite al-Zarqawi to join al-Qaeda outright.

Although both al-Zarqawi and bin Laden founded dangerous extremist Muslim institutions, their lives had almost nothing in common. Bin Laden was a college graduate from a very wealthy and influential family; al-Zarqawi was fired from a job as a cashier and born into a small family in a run-down neighborhood.

Ahmad Fadhil Nazzal al-Khalaylah was born in a poor part of the industrial city of Zarqa, Jordan. Zarqa is Jordan's third largest city and a destination for Islamic radicals. It is from the name of this city that Ahmad took the name al-Zarqawi. He felt a lot of affection for his hometown; until he died, he kept a house in Zarqa, asking his sisters to check on it from time to time. When his mother died of leukemia in 2004, he returned to Zarqa in disguise to attend her funeral, even though he was the most wanted man in Jordan.

Troublemaker

Al-Zarqawi was a wild teenager. He had the reputation of a bully and a thug. He was a heavy drinker and was constantly getting into fights. When he was 15, he robbed a relative's home. He dropped out of high school in his final year. In order to stop his destructive habits, al-Zarqawi's mother enrolled him in religious education at a local mosque. It was here that al-Zarqawi learned about Salafism. This is a teaching that emphasizes that Islam needs to return to the purity and traditions of Muhammad and accuses the West and democracy of polluting the Muslim world.

Despite his mother's best efforts, al-Zarqawi grew up to become a petty criminal. He did drugs and was covered in tattoos, including a distinctive green tattoo on his left hand. He was in and out of prison many times.

THE DEADLY SURGEON

Ayman al-Zawahiri was an Egyptian surgeon who became one of Osama bin Laden's most trusted advisors. He was born into a prominent Egyptian family in Cairo. He was arrested at 16 for joining the Muslim Brotherhood and again when he was 30, this time on a weapons charge. Al-Zawahiri joined the Egyptian Islamic Jihad organization and was active in extreme Islamic violence from a young age. In prison, he was a sort of spokesman for imprisoned Islamic extremists. He left for Pakistan in 1985 to help treat Afghani fighters waging war against the Soviets. It was there that he met Osama bin Laden.

Ayman al-Zawahiri was a surgeon and became a top official in al-Qaeda. After bin Laden's death in 2011, he was named the leader of al-Qaeda.

In 1989, al-Zarqawi arrived in Khost, Afghanistan, and stayed for three years, establishing contacts. He was hired as the correspondent for a jihadist magazine called *Al Bonian al Marsous*, or *The Strong Wall*. Al-Zarqawi's reports consisted of interviews with veterans of the Soviet-Afghan war. Eventually, he began attending training camps on the Afghanistan-Pakistan border. According to bin Laden's former bodyguard, these camps were made up of three phases. These phases consisted of 15 days of psychological exhaustion, followed by 45 days of learning how to handle weapons, and ended with military theory.

Al-Maqdisi

Al-Zarqawi returned to Jordan in 1992 and was introduced to Abu Muhammad al-Maqdisi, an intelligent Jordanian-Palestinian Salafist who had recently published a particularly aggressive anti-West paper. Al-Maqdisi practiced the most extreme version of Salafism, which was based on hatred of Shia and Western cultures and literal interpretation of the Koran. (It was actually similar to the Wahhabism of Saudi Arabia that Osama bin Laden studied.) Al-Maqdisi became al-Zarqawi's mentor and a tremendous influence.

The research director of the Combating Terrorism Center at West Point, Jarret Brachman, said,

It's not surprising that Zarqawi em-
braced Salafism. Jihadi Salafism is
black and white—and so is every-
thing that Zarqawi's ever done. When
he met al-Maqdisi, he was drifting,
trying to find an outlet, and very im-
pressionable [easy to influence]. His
religious grounding, until then, was
largely dependent upon whose influ-
ence he was under at the time. And
since his father had died when he was
young, he'd been seeking a father fig-
ure. Al-Maqdisi served both needs.[3]

In Jordan, al-Maqdisi preached and recruited while al-Zarqawi met Abu Muntassir, an experienced Islamic militant. Muntassir remembers al-Zarqawi as a rookie who was very eager to learn more about Islam and how to wage jihad. Muntassir would end up teaching al-Zarqawi much about the religion. He recounted, "Zarqawi asked me to work with him in an Islamic group; al-Maqdisi was already on board. The idea was there, but it had no leadership and no name."[4] The group that al-Zarqawi, al-Maqdisi, and Muntassir formed consisted of about a dozen men who aimed to overthrow the Jordanian monarchy and establish an Islamic government. However, it was not yet a well-oiled machine.

Prison or University?

This group called itself Bayat al-Imam, which means Allegiance to the Imam. (An imam is a high-ranking Muslim religious official.) Its first attempt at terrorism was in Zarqa in 1993. The group sent one of their men to blow up a local movie theater because it was showing inappropriate films. This bomber, however, was distracted by the film and ended up blowing his own legs off. This was not the group's only failure. In 1994, the Jordanian military raided al-Zarqawi's family home and found a stockpile of weapons, including grenades. Charged with possession of illegal weapons and belonging to a terrorist organization, he was sentenced to 15 years in Jordan's Swaqa Prison.

The Jordanian military, shown here, was able to keep al-Zarqawi controlled and even had him in prison before he was able to escape into Afghanistan.

The time he spent in prison shaped al-Zarqawi into the man who would establish ISIS years later. He held a lot of authority over other prisoners. A counterterrorism official from the Pentagon claimed, "prison was [al-Zarqawi's] university."[5] It is where he made connections and developed credibility as a radical Islamic leader. Under the guidance of al-Maqdisi, he did his best to memorize the verses of the Koran— all 6,236 of them. New recruits were drawn to him—some because they were curious and others because they were afraid.

A fellow prisoner of al-Zarqawi's, Abdullah Abu Rumman, said that al-Zarqawi controlled the prison ward: "He decided who would cook, who would do the laundry, who would lead the readings of the Koran. He was extremely protective of his followers, and extremely tough with the prisoners outside the group. He didn't trust them. He considered them infidels."[6]

Its leaders being in prison did not slow the growth of Bayat al-Imam; it expanded both inside and outside the prison. Al-Zarqawi recruited, and al-Maqdisi preached. They used the Internet to spread their message across continents. Al-Maqdisi's sermons were smuggled out of Swaqa by prisoners' wives and mothers with help from prison guards. They were then posted on Salafist and jihadist websites. Al-Zarqawi even wrote a few sermons himself. These came to the attention of Osama bin Laden.

In 1999, Jordan's king died, and his son pardoned more than 3,000 prisoners. After serving just five years of his sentence, al-Zarqawi was freed.

Al-Zarqawi and al-Qaeda

After his release from Swaqa, al-Zarqawi once again found himself in Afghanistan, picking up where he left off. In December of that year, he first met Osama bin Laden at the Government Guest House in the city of Kandahar, the capital of the Taliban. A former Israeli intelligence official described it as "loathing at first sight."[7] Al-Zarqawi's tattoos made bin Laden see him as a thug who might be a spy for the Jordanian government. Moreover, al-Zarqawi's hatred for Shiites also struck bin Laden as problematic—bin Laden's own mother was from a Shia sect. Al-Zarqawi was rejected as a candidate for real membership in al-Qaeda.

Although bin Laden still did not completely trust al-Zarqawi's prejudices against fellow Muslims, his advisors convinced him that a partnership would be beneficial. After all, al-Zarqawi had contacts in Jordan, Syria, and Lebanon that could be useful to al-Qaeda. In 2000, al-Zarqawi was given $5,000 to develop a training camp in Herat, Afghanistan. Herat is Afghanistan's third largest city and lies right on the border with Iran. It was there that al-Zarqawi attracted jihadists from Palestine, Syria, Lebanon, and Turkey.

By 2001, al-Zarqawi had evolved from an unsophisticated thug into a

SEPTEMBER 11, 2001

As al-Zarqawi was developing his followers, bin Laden and al-Qaeda were carrying out a devastating attack on U.S. soil. After the suicide attacks on September 11, 2001, bin Laden went on Arab television and told all Muslims that they were either infidels or believers. This was the first time he claimed responsibility for a terrorist attack: "We calculated in advance the number of casualties from the enemy, who would be killed based on the position of the tower. We calculated that the floors that would be hit would be three or four floors. I was the most optimistic of them all."[1]

Al-Qaeda's attack on the United States in 2001 killed more than 3,000 people.

1. Quoted in Kate Zernike and Michael T. Kaufman, "The Most Wanted Face of Terrorism," *New York Times*, May 2, 2011. www.nytimes.com/2011/05/02/world/02osama-bin-laden-obituary.html.

military commander. He was inspired by the figure of Nur al-Din, a medieval ruler who held lands from Syria to Iraq. He had driven off Christian crusaders and united Muslim leaders. Historians think that al-Din's empire is what inspired al-Zarqawi to travel to Iraq after the fall of the Islamic Emirate in Afghanistan. The Taliban established the Islamic Emirate in Afghanistan in 1996. It strictly enforced Islamic law and gave shelter to jihadist groups. It collapsed when the United States bombed the city of Kandahar, killing Osama bin Laden's military planner and ending the Taliban's rule in Afghanistan. After this fall, al-Zarqawi fled for Iran but later decided that Iraq would be a better place for his group of jihadists to blend in. He strongly believed that the United States would invade Iraq, and he would play an important and necessary role in the resistance.

The United States Gives al-Zarqawi a Boost

As al-Zarqawi was getting to Iraq, on the other side of the world, he was being recognized by the United States as a growing threat. The Central Intelligence Agency (CIA) knew exactly where al-Zarqawi was, and they proposed that he be targeted in order to prevent any future problems. They created a plan of attack that would take al-Zarqawi out of the picture for good. They were shocked when President George Bush and Vice President Dick Cheney did not approve their action. Vice President Cheney, it appeared, wanted to use al-Zarqawi as a link between Osama bin Laden and Saddam Hussein.

Saddam Hussein was the dictator of Iraq and a Sunni Muslim. He became the president in 1979 and, sharing al-Zarqawi's feelings about Shia Muslims, expelled 40,000 of them from the country. Until the fall of Iraq in 2003 and his execution in 2006, Hussein continued a reign of terror and death against his own Iraqi people. He was known around the world for attempting to develop nuclear and biological weapons. After the September 11, 2001, terror attacks, the White House tried to link Hussein to the violence, but they were unable to.

In 2003, al-Zarqawi was entering Iraq with a history of terrorism and a strong link to al-Qaeda. To some U.S. government officials, he seemed like the link between Afghanistan-based al-Qaeda and the Iraqi leader.

The two biggest problems with this theory were that al-Zarqawi had barely worked under Osama bin Laden and had never worked with Saddam Hussein. There was no connection at all between him and what happened on September 11, 2001. Regardless, citizens of the United States were outraged after the tragic attacks happened on American soil, and the government was looking for an excuse to send in soldiers. Just like that, al-Zarqawi became the link to justify putting troops in Iraq.

Saddam Hussein, pictured here, was the president of Iraq from 1979 to 2003. His rule is remembered for being brutal and oppressive.

In February 2003, Colin Powell, the U.S. Secretary of State at the time, gave a speech to the United Nations (UN) describing the Iraqi weapons program headed by Saddam Hussein. The extent of this weapons program and the amount of danger it actually posed is still debated. Regardless, this speech directly mentioned al-Zarqawi as the link between al-Qaeda in Afghanistan and those weapons in Iraq. Members of the CIA helped write the speech, wanting to emphasize the fact that they did not have any evidence linking al-Zarqawi and Hussein. After leaving their hands, however, the speech was changed by members of the vice president's office. The final version that Secretary Powell delivered included seven minutes focused directly on al-Zarqawi. This minor jihadist who had been turned away by al-Qaeda was suddenly world-famous. Secretary Powell has since stated that he should have double-checked the facts of this speech, and he considers it a permanent stain on his record.

In the days following this speech, al-Zarqawi disappeared from U.S. view. The United States publicly disbanded Iraq's military in 2003. The 250,000 former soldiers were unhappy with their sudden unemployment. They began to protest, and violence eventually broke out. Al-Zarqawi took advantage of this situation to recruit Muslims with combat training to his extremist cause. These protests marked the beginning of al-Zarqawi using suicide bombers to cause destruction, confusion, and fear in Iraq. In one of his most infamous attacks, he sent a suicide bomber to the UN headquarters in Iraq. This grabbed the attention of the United States. The CIA quickly released a statement to the president that said al-Zarqawi was leading an organized uprising, and White House officials did not like this information. The CIA's claims were then supported by al-Zarqawi himself. In one of the most brutal messages of the war, he personally beheaded a prisoner and posted the video online.

The man al-Zarqawi killed was an American freelance radio tower repairman named Nicholas Berg. Richard Clarke, former National Coordinator for Counterterrorism in the United States, emphasized that al-Zarqawi killing with his own two hands made him very appealing to the younger Islamic extremists.

The U.S. government reacted by declaring a $25 million bounty on al-Zarqawi's head—around the same price offered for the capture of bin Laden. He was branded one of America's greatest enemies and was well on his way to earning his nickname: the Sheikh (king) of the Slaughterers.

Al-Zarqawi Enters Iraq

Al-Zarqawi arrived in Iraq in June 2003 with his new terrorist group named Jama'at al-Tawhid wa al-Jihad (Monotheism and Jihad). By August, his group had bombed the Jordanian embassy and the UN headquarters in Baghdad.

Colin Powell's speech at the UN in 2003 made al-Zarqawi famous across the world.

In those two attacks alone, more than 30 people were killed and at least 65 were wounded. He also bombed the mosque of Imam Ali, one of Iraq's holiest Shia shrines, killing more than 80 civilians while they prayed. Al-Zarqawi saw the Shia as servants of evil who would fight against the Sunni Muslims at the time of the apocalypse.

Al-Zarqawi taught his followers that many different acts could separate a Muslim from Islam, such as selling drugs, wearing Western clothes, shaving one's beard, or voting in an election (even for a Muslim candidate). He believed that putting any man-made law above the laws made by Allah was punishable by death. He believed that the Shia did exactly this, which meant that about 200 million Muslims deserved to die, along with the heads of state of every Islamic country in the world.

Although the United States had portrayed al-Zarqawi as the link between al-Qaeda and Iraq, once al-Zarqawi expanded in Iraq, he started to lose al-Qaeda. His old spiritual mentor from Jordan, al-Maqdisi, was an important intellectual member of al-Qaeda. He was increasingly disappointed with al-Zarqawi's extreme violence. Al-Qaeda considered it a sin for al-Zarqawi to hate and kill other Muslims. He was spreading too much *takfir*, which means excommunication or being rejected by the faith. Al-Maqdisi urged his former friend to focus his fight on Americans instead.

Al-Zarqawi, however, continued to murder Shia by the hundreds.

When al-Zarqawi blew up the Shia shrine and attracted the support of Sunnis in Iraq, a civil war was sparked that would kill tens of thousands of people. Al-Zarqawi counted on the Sunnis to resent the Shia, and with his encouragement, they did. He sent dozens of Sunni suicide bombers to blow up mosques, schools, and markets in Shia neighborhoods. Al-Zarqawi then took his mission a step further than bin Laden ever had. He deliberately showed his face to the world in a video posted online. In this video, he claimed that he would create an Islamic State and it would be the fulfillment of a prophecy—the prophecy that called for the end of the world. This apocalyptic message would later serve as the centerpiece of ISIS's brutal terrorist methodology.

Al-Qaeda in Iraq

In late 2004, al-Zarqawi agreed to join al-Qaeda. He did not want to join the organization because its members were not extreme enough for him. Nevertheless, motivated by the extra power that would come with being associated with al-Qaeda, he joined with them and took the title Emir (prince) of al-Qaeda's Operations in the Land of the Two Rivers (Iraq). This was the beginning of al-Qaeda in Iraq, or AQI. However, bin Laden quickly saw how different al-Zarqawi's approach to terrorism was from his own.

He did not care about popular public opinion or projecting a positive image. Al-Qaeda was sure the general Muslim public would reject his actions. Al-Zarqawi simply did not care; he wrote,

If we are able to strike [the Shia] with one painful blow after another until they enter the battle ... Then, no value or influence will remain to the Governing Council or even to the Americans, who will enter a second battle with the [Shia]. This is what we want, and, whether they like it or not, many Sunni areas will stand with the mujahidin [jihadists].[8]

This attitude was concerning for top members of al-Qaeda. Bin Laden's right hand man, al-Zawahiri, wrote in 2005 that the jihadists "shouldn't stir questions in the hearts and minds of the people about the benefit of our actions ... we are in a media battle in a race for the hearts and minds of our [Muslim] community."[9] Al-Qaeda believed that al-Zarqawi would burn himself out and destroy his own vision through his enthusiasm for violence and tendency to murder his own people. They told him he must consult with them before making any strategic decisions.

By 2006, al-Zarqawi saw himself as a commander and spiritual leader for Sunni Muslim people across the globe. He now had influence over people, and as the leader of AQI, he had real power over Iraqi citizens. He demanded that all Sunnis follow his interpretation of sharia law: All women would wear veils, and all criminals would be beheaded—even prominent figures in the community were publicly executed if they showed any resistance to al-Zarqawi's rule.

Then, on June 7, 2006, the U.S. Air Force dropped a pair of huge bombs on al-Zarqawi's hideout, located 20 miles (32 km) north of Baghdad. Al-Qaeda in Iraq's leader, the Sheikh of the Slaughterers who had murdered hundreds of innocents, was killed.

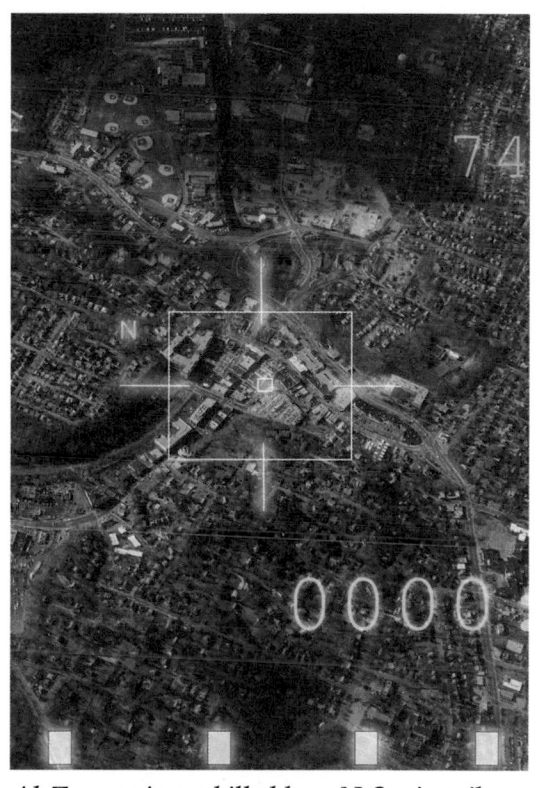

Al-Zarqawi was killed by a U.S. airstrike in 2006. This dealt AQI a great blow.

CHAPTER TWO

AL-MASRI
AND THE CREATION OF
THE ISLAMIC STATE

From Osama bin Laden to Abu Musab al-Zarqawi, terrorist activity in the Middle East had been on the rise for decades. In the 1990s and the early 2000s, countries such as the United States viewed al-Qaeda as their biggest threat. After all, the September 11, 2001, attacks on American soil had been planned and carried out by its soldiers, and it was responsible for thousands of deaths. However, bin Laden's group would soon be overshadowed. After Colin Powell's speech to the UN, al-Zarqawi became a terrorist celebrity, and he used his new power and influence to build a strong organization in Iraq and Syria. Even after his death, their activities not only carried on—they eventually even increased.

The new leaders of AQI faced resistance from government-paid fighters. Intervention from the United States led to a decrease in terrorist sympathizers for a few years, and it looked like AQI was on the brink of destruction. Throughout it all, however, its members kept up their violent activities, even if they were now on a smaller scale. After a brief period of relative peace, the American military believed it had done enough to stabilize the region, and they withdrew troops from the country. Abuses by the new Iraqi government, however, would lead to the creation of an even greater enemy: ISIS.

The Sons of Iraq

As al-Zarqawi's hideout was being bombed by the United States, many Sunni groups began to revolt against AQI. Al-Zarqawi's belief in strict adherence to sharia laws was not making life easy for followers of any denomination of Islam in Iraq.

The U.S. military saw this as an opportunity. General David Petraeus organized and financed a revolt against AQI that became known as the Awakening. Any Sunnis who were willing to fight against AQI, even if they had previously fought against the Americans on behalf of Saddam Hussein, were recruited for this effort and called the Sons of Iraq. This nickname was meant to unite the individual tribes under one national banner and to bring attention to the fact that most of AQI's leaders were foreigners, such as al-Zarqawi, who was from Jordan. These Sunnis believed that joining forces with the United States would spare them from punishment for previous crimes they had committed as part of Saddam Hussein's military.

United States Army General David Petraeus helped organize Iraqis to fight against AQI. His Awakening strategy allowed the U.S. military to begin its exit from the country.

Iraqi Prime Minister Nouri al-Maliki did not keep his promises after the United States left Iraq. He is pictured here with President George W. Bush.

The United States came to Iraq with the intention of bringing stability to the country and its people. However, Iraq did not necessarily embrace yet another foreign force attempting to control its territory. The Awakening was designed to stop some of the violence and give the United States a window during which it could leave. It was not designed to help repair the hatred between the Shia

and the Sunnis that al-Zarqawi had encouraged. This responsibility was left to Iraq's elected Shia government and Prime Minister Nouri al-Maliki. Al-Maliki, however, failed to keep the peace. The Sons of Iraq were not given the salaries or the government contracts they were promised, Sunni politicians were humiliated and fired, and the police and military were promptly filled with Shia members. His rule aggravated the wounds already caused by the previous decade of war.

The Islamic State

Despite the death of al-Zarqawi and the resistance from Iraqi tribes, AQI had not totally disappeared. Not long after their leader was killed in 2006, al-Zarqawi's successor tried to bring the jihadists back together. This man was named Abu Ayyub al-Masri. The organization of extremists changed its name from al-Qaeda in Iraq to the Islamic State of Iraq, or ISI. To strengthen his leadership, al-Masri named Abu Omar al-Baghdadi as the commander of the faithful. This was the highest rank in the organization. Other jihadists thought this was strange, as they had ever heard of Abu Omar. Nevertheless, he became a prominent figure of ISI alongside al-Masri for several years.

The Islamic State chose its new name purposefully to be mysterious. Jihadists more commonly used the word emirate than state to describe a small area of land. In Arabic, the word for state is *dawla*. This word not only means a modern nation, it also brings up a feeling of medieval caliphates such as Dawla Abbasiyya. This legendary *dawla* covered the land over Mesopotamia, the Persian Gulf, and North Africa with Islamic rule.

The change of name confused the supporters of al-Qaeda. Was the Islamic State trying to break away from AQI? Many extremists wondered how they were expected to pledge allegiance to the unknown Abu Omar when they had already pledged their allegiance to

Mullah Omar, the head of the Taliban. Moreover, the decision to change the name and announce the Islamic State was done without consulting bin Laden. This caused a major break between ISI and al-Qaeda.

Al-Masri's Regime

Although Abu Omar was named the commander of the faithful, the real new leader of the Islamic State was Abu Ayyub al-Masri (sometimes known as Abu Hamza al-Muhajir). Al-Masri was an Egyptian who, in 1982, joined a group named Islamic Jihad in his home country. This organization was run by Osama bin Laden's future associate, Ayman al-Zawahiri. During the time he spent in this organization, he became an expert in explosives. It was around this time that al-Masri met al-Zarqawi, with whom he went to Iraq. Al-Zarqawi put him in charge of recruiting suicide bombers. Because of his close association with al-Zarqawi, al-Masri was chosen to lead what remained of AQI after the death of its former leader. One of his first public moves was to definitively declare that the terrorist organization would continue to fight Shia Muslims and Western troops. Al-Masri is most famous for renaming AQI the Islamic State of Iraq.

Al-Masri knew he needed to appoint a commander of the faithful for the new Islamic State. His first step was to find the perfect man for the role. He eventually decided on Abu Omar al-Baghdadi, who was originally known as

Hamid al-Zawi, a former police officer from a small farming town. Al-Zawi was fired from the police force in the early 1990s for his extremely conservative religious views. He lived a relatively simple life in Baghdad until the Americans invaded Iraq in 2003. He then joined AQI and later the Islamic State. He also took the name Abu Omar al-Baghdadi in an attempt to emphasize that he lived in Baghdad. His appointment to leader of the organization seemed to be based on nothing.

Al-Masri gave Abu Omar this position for three reasons. First, he wanted to reinforce the fact that ISI was a strict Islamic group. Second, the Islamic State needed to be structured like a real government, and the commander of the faithful was its head. The third, and most important, reason Abu Omar was given his position is because he was easy to manipulate. Al-Masri was the real person in power.

Al-Qaeda leaders began to worry that the Islamic State was going to distance itself from their rule. However, al-Masri claimed that the State had kept its pledge of allegiance to bin Laden, just not publicly. He claimed that this was to keep the peace and encourage Iraqis to think of them as separate organizations. Al-Masri wanted to improve the image of the Islamic State and not have it associated with a terrorist group. Throughout this time, al-Masri was building up the government for his State. He reassigned terrorists to the Army of the State (a new name for their army). In 2006, al-Masri named himself the Minister of War in the Islamic State's first cabinet.

All of these moves help identify al-Masri as someone who had big-picture politics in mind. Rather than just the brutal violence of al-Zarqawi, he wanted to build the new Islamic world. Al-Masri still accomplished this by murdering hundreds of innocent people, but his eventual plan was to truly expand the Islamic State into a global caliphate. Some modern observers have pointed this out as the major difference between al-Masri and al-Zarqawi. Both men were incredibly dangerous and willing to murder as many people as they needed to, but al-Zarqawi did not have any real plans to establish his caliphate. Al-Masri was always working toward this end goal.

Many jihadists were critical of this new leadership. Some said that the Islamic State had no land, so it failed to meet the requirements of a real Islamic state. Most of the Sunni groups protested because they only wanted to liberate Iraq, not create an Islamic state. Additionally, ISI had challenged the authority of bin Laden and al-Qaeda. Many of their fighters were loyal to bin Laden and his organization. Although it was not happy with the defiance of ISI, al-Qaeda publicly endorsed the establishment of the Islamic State. As bin Laden's trusted advisor, al-Zawahiri wrote in December 2007,

I want to clarify that there is noth-

ing in Iraq by the name of al-Qaeda. Rather, the organization of [al-Qaeda in Iraq] merged, by the grace of God, with other jihadist groups in the Islamic State of Iraq, may God protect it. It is a legitimate emirate established on a legitimate and sound method. It was established through consultation and won the oath of allegiance from most of the mujahids [terrorists] and tribes in Iraq.[10]

The Mahdi

One reason ISI was able to keep a lot of fighters faithful is because they scared people. One way of doing this was by bringing up the Mahdi. This figure is similar to Jesus Christ in Christian traditions. The history of this Islamic hero goes back to the ancient world.

In the seventh and eighth centuries, the Umayyad dynasty ruled the Islamic empire from the ancient city of Damascus, Syria. They had taken over the caliphate from the Prophet Muhammad's son-in-law and grandsons, which made many Muslims angry. Rumors then started about a man from the prophet's

family who would bring justice to Islam and destruction to its enemies. The rumors called this Islamic savior the Mahdi, which means rightly guided. The first man who used the Mahdi as a political tool was al-Mukhtar ibn Abu Ubayd al-Thaqafi. Born in the seventh century, he led a revolutionary rebellion against the Umayyad caliphate in Iraq. He taught his followers that they needed to overthrow the government to prepare the world for the Mahdi.

This savior figure was important for many Muslims because he would supposedly signal that the apocalypse was near. He was described as being the leader of Islam's armies in the world's final battle. The prophecies about the Mahdi were not found in the Koran but in volumes called *ahadith*. These were written many years after the Prophet Muhammad's death. They tend to reflect the political and cultural ideas of the time they were written, rather than the true ideals of Islam.

In the 21st century, the Islamic State has taken advantage of the Mahdi to proclaim that they are fighting a good fight. They bring up the apocalypse and

FROM NO ONE TO THE COMMANDER OF THE FAITHFUL

Unlike al-Zarqawi, who spent years building his reputation as head of al-Qaeda in Iraq, Abu Omar al-Baghdadi was a man with a much lower reputation. He had not been associated with any high-profile attacks or murders. Moreover, Abu Omar rarely appeared in any videos and when he did, only his voice was recorded. His face was never revealed publicly. It is presumed that this was for security reasons. However, because he never appeared publicly and al-Masri controlled ISI, some doubted that Abu Omar existed at all—until his dead body proved that he did.

IMPROVISED EXPLOSIVE DEVICES

ISIS uses a wide range of improvised explosive devices (IEDs) to kill and scare victims. They are considered to be improvised because they regularly take the form of common objects and are used as traps for soldiers or Shiites. Some of the most common are vehicle-borne improvised explosive devices (VBIEDs). These are incredibly dangerous because a suicide bomber can drive into a crowded space and detonate a large amount of explosives, or ISIS can abandon a vehicle on a highway that will explode when soldiers or others investigate it. These surprise attacks are one reason that ISIS seems to have a lot of military strength. IEDs are effective at killing or injuring many people at once, and they are inexpensive to produce.

Car bombs are very deadly, and they frighten people by making everyday objects into lethal weapons.

the Mahdi as a way of controlling their followers and recruiting more.

Under al-Masri's Rule

Although he attempted to unite Muslims under his single black flag, al-Masri was a bad leader. In 2006, at the beginning of his Islamic State career, the U.S. government offered a $5 million bounty for information about his location; by 2008, they were offering only $100,000. Al-Masri often did not know what his subordinates were doing, and he was very far removed from the reality of the State's actions.

Sunnis who tried to resist the Islamic State were told they could either join or hand over their weapons. The State began kidnapping and executing resistors to demonstrate its power over Iraqi citizens. Another radical group, named the Islamic Army, was hit particularly hard by this crackdown. They refused to bow to the Islamic State, so the State killed 30 of its members, despite knowing it was destroying a chance for an alliance with another group with similar interests.

Although he was the leader of a large organization, al-Masri continued to demonstrate his inability to manage the Islamic State. The Islamic State's bullying and murdering caused other militant groups to ask the Americans to destroy it. Complaints were written to al-Qaeda in Afghanistan concerning the division in Iraq. The Sunnis in particular were losing patience.

The al-Masri Slump

In November 2007, a man named Abu Sulayman al-Utaybi was removed from his position as the chief sharia law judge of the Islamic State because of disagreements with al-Masri. Shortly afterward, he approached al-Qaeda to accuse al-Masri of running the Islamic State poorly. Al-Qaeda was worried that al-Masri had too much power without anyone to contain it. Abu Omar al-Baghdadi had a high position, but al-Utaybi claimed he was just al-Masri's puppet, and al-Qaeda was unsure of what would happen if al-Masri were to die. They reached out to Abu Omar himself but received no answer. Al-Masri was then summoned to answer to al-Qaeda's leaders. Meanwhile, his accuser, al-Utaybi, was killed by U.S. forces.

It was a bad time for the cause of the Islamic State, which was good for the rest of Iraq. In early 2007, roughly 2,500 civilians were killed each month. By the end of 2008, this number had been reduced to 500 per month. Although these deaths were still tragic, Iraq's Sunni tribes were starting to contain the Islamic State while the United States got rid of its leadership. This damaged the Islamic State's reputation: Jihadists could not believe that the Islamic State had Allah's support if it was being defeated by outsiders. Many still referred to the Islamic State as al-Qaeda in Iraq,

THE ISLAMIC STATE FLAG

In an effort to prove its legitimate statehood, shortly after being established, the Islamic State revealed its flag. It is black with white letters stating, in Arabic, "No god but God," and underneath that, it features a white circle with black lettering that reads, "Muhammad is the Messenger of God." These messages are written in ragged lettering that looks handwritten despite being designed on a computer. This is to make people think of an era that predates technology. The Islamic State uses this flag as a symbol to unify people. In early Islam, the color black was associated with revenge for a wrongful death. According to history, those loyal to the Prophet Muhammad wore black to avenge those who persecuted his family. A black flag is a symbol of vengeance on Muslim rulers who went against the Prophet Muhammad. ISIS also believes that this is the flag that all Muslims should follow when the end of the world comes.

Even though the Islamic State flag was designed on a computer, it looks handwritten on purpose.

so this bad reputation reflected on the original al-Qaeda in Afghanistan. However, bin Laden still refused to denounce the Islamic State.

A joint American-Iraqi raid in April 2010 brought the death of both Abu Ayyub al-Masri and Abu Omar al-Baghdadi. Over the next 3 months, 34 more Islamic State leaders were either killed or captured. In May 2010, a man named Abu Bakr al-Baghdadi was appointed as the Islamic State's new commander of the faithful. Just as with Abu Omar, few jihadists had ever heard of him. It would be two years before he would make a public appearance.

CHAPTER THREE

ABU BAKR AL-BAGHDADI

When the United States killed Abu Musab al-Zarqawi, they thought they had won a major victory in the war on terror. They were unfortunately incorrect; his successors took power almost immediately and continued his violence. Under the leadership of Abu Ayyub al-Masri and Abu Omar al-Baghdadi, AQI disappeared. It was replaced by ISI, which would later evolve into ISIS. However, because of this name and leadership change, ISI and al-Qaeda were beginning to fight with each other. Because Osama bin Laden was in hiding and the rulers of the Islamic State were weak, neither side was able to grow much between 2006 and 2010. This changed, though, after the deaths of al-Masri and Abu Omar.

As their new leader, Abu Bakr al-Baghdadi, rose to his position, the power of the Islamic State rose as well. It expanded operations, recruited more fighters than ever, and spread its corruption across the globe using social media.

The background of al-Baghdadi's life, including how he rose to his high position in ISIS, highlights the intense and complicated social environment of Iraq and the Middle East. The feud between Sunni and Shia Muslims is more than 1,000 years old, and recent attacks from both sides have not helped the relationship between the two Islamic sects. As of 2016, al-Baghdadi has been the most successful leader of terrorists in Iraq and Syria. Success for a radical jihadist means destroying thousands of lives.

Another al-Baghdadi

Ibrahim Awwad Ibrahim al-Badri was 39 when he assumed the name al-Baghdadi and the Islamic State position of commander of the faithful. He was born in 1971 to a lower–middle class Sunni farming family in Samarra, Iraq. His father, Awwad, was religious and taught recitation of the Koran in the local mosque. Awwad was proud of his lineage, claiming to be a descendant from the Prophet Muhammad.

Some of al-Badri's family were members of Iraq's Baath Party, which was a socialist political party focused on creating a pan-Arab union, which meant that they wanted to join all Arabic nations together as a whole. Baathist leaders tolerated private religion but discouraged activism because

Few people had ever heard of Abu Bakr al-Baghdadi when he became the leader of the Islamic State in 2010. Unlike al-Masri, he has proven to be an effective terrorist leader.

it was a distraction from their goal of unification. Baathism dominated Iraqi politics, and anyone who wanted a government job needed to join the party. Two of al-Badri's uncles served in Saddam Hussein's government, and two of his brothers joined the army. Al-Badri himself had bad eyesight, which kept him home.

The al-Badri family is an example of how Iraqis had to shift allegiances in order to survive Saddam Hussein's dictatorship. They had ties to the powerful Baathist party while also keeping ties to Salafism, the exact example of extremism that Baathists discouraged. Saddam Hussein saw Salafis as a threat because they wanted states to impose Islamic, rather than nonreligious, law. Many Salafis were jailed during his rule. However, if Saddam Hussein wanted to remain in power, he did need the support of religious conservatives. Therefore, he started a Faith Campaign, imposing harsh punishments for crimes. These punishments came directly from Islamic scriptures. The most famous of these punishments is cutting off a thief's hand. As a major component of the Faith Campaign, people were encouraged to study and recite the Koran. Iraq used state funds to train 30,000 new teachers of the holy text.

"The Believer"

While these major religious and political changes were happening around him, the young al-Badri remained quiet and devout. His friends and neighbors gave him a nickname: "the believer." He was shy and serious, even while playing soccer. He never excelled at his studies, but he was good at memorizing and reciting verses from the Koran, just like his father. When he was not at school, he was at the local mosque. Even among friends and family, he was quick to scold anyone who did not strictly follow Islamic law. Al-Badri wanted to study law at the University of Baghdad, but because his high school grades were not good, he studied the Koran instead.

After his undergraduate education, al-Badri enrolled in the new Saddam

SADDAM HUSSEIN'S ISLAMIC SUPPORT

Hussein was concerned with appearing to support the passionately religious citizens of Iraq. In addition to instituting some aspects of sharia law, he also encouraged more builders to construct mosques as part of his Faith Campaign. He built one of these mosques as a memorial to his military victories in the 1990s. Taken from one of Hussein's speeches, it was named the Mother of All Battles Mosque. He claimed to have donated a huge amount of his own blood to be used as ink for the Koran that would be kept there on display. It totals 605 pages and was displayed from 2001 to 2003.

SOCCER AND SALAFISM

Between 2000 and 2004, not much is known about al-Badri's activities. Reports show that he had two wives and six children. His first wife was his cousin. He and his growing family did not socialize much. He taught recitation of the Koran at the neighborhood mosque. The mosque also had a soccer club, on which al-Badri was the star player. The other players and spectators sometimes called him Messi, referencing Argentinian soccer player Lionel Messi. However, teammates reported that when he missed a goal, he would lose his temper. As a radical Salafist, he also lost his temper whenever he saw behavior that he considered un-Islamic. This obsession with maintaining a strict Muslim code would foreshadow his leadership of ISIS.

University for Islamic Studies, where he wrote a masters thesis on medieval commentary on the Koran. Upon finishing this in 1999, he immediately continued on in the Koranic studies doctoral program. During graduate school, his uncle, Ismail al-Badri, convinced him to join a Salafist group: the Muslim Brotherhood. This was the same organization that Osama bin Laden had joined before founding al-Qaeda.

The goal of the Muslim Brotherhood was to establish Islamic governments.

Most branches of the Brotherhood were peaceful. Some members were liberal, and others were conservative, but they all cooperated. Most Salafis are not jihadists and reject organizations such as al-Qaeda and ISIS. They focus their commitment on expanding the land of Islam through their own devoted worship and personal observance. To most Salafis, starting a war is completely forbidden. Wars interrupt prayer and appropriate worship. Most Salafis also believe that Muslims should remove themselves from politics. Radical Salafism, however, ignores these rules. Like al-Zarqawi before him, al-Badri associated with the ultraconservative Salafi members in Baghdad. He considered the mainstream Brotherhood to be made up of "people of words, not action."[11]

Prisons Make Good Neighbors

After the Americans had overpowered Saddam Hussein's army in 2003, al-Badri helped develop a rebel group that fought the U.S. troops and their allies in Iraq. This group was called Jaysh Ahl al-Sunna wa-l-Jamaah, or the Army of the People of the Sunna and Communal Solidarity.

In February 2004, while visiting a friend who was on the U.S. most wanted list in Fallujah, Iraq, al-Badri was arrested by the U.S. military for being associated with the extreme Salafis. He was held for nearly a year at the prison Camp Bucca as a civilian detainee. This

The flag of the Muslim Brotherhood represented efforts to expand Islam that were generally peaceful.

meant that the Americans were unable to officially associate him with an insurgent terrorist group. His jailers did not know he was a jihadist.

Much like al-Zarqawi before him, al-Badri was shaped by his time in prison. He stayed serious, led prayers, and conducted religious classes. He even had the opportunity to impress everyone on the soccer field. Although he was quiet, he fit in with the different groups of inmates to win support and negotiate between rival groups. One of his fellow prisoners remembered: "Every time there was a problem in the camp, he was at the center of it. He wanted to be the head of the prison—and when I look back now, he was using a policy of conquer and divide to get what he wanted, which was status. And it worked."[12]

The United States did not know it, but Camp Bucca became a cultivation center for jihadist beliefs and thoughts. Many inmates were Sunnis who had served Saddam Hussein, and though few were jihadists when they arrived at Bucca, many were when they left. A prisoner named Abu Ahmed, who knew al-Badri, said, "We could never have all got together like this in Baghdad, or anywhere else. It would have been impossibly dangerous. Here, [in prison] we were not only safe, but we were only a few hundred metres away from the entire [al-Qaeda] leadership."[13]

These prisons became known as "jihadi universities" because a large number of people with similar interests were creating new networks. Through inmates connected to al-Qaeda, al-Badri learned of al-Zarqawi and his methods. For al-Badri, this was a tremendous opportunity to make connections and friends with former members of Saddam Hussein's army—friends who would later happily join the Islamic State. They reconnected after release from prison by writing one another's phone numbers in the elastic of their underwear.

FROM PRISON TO POWER

After he was released from prison, al-Badri joined al-Qaeda in Iraq, drawn to its extremist views of Islam. Since there were not many academic religious scholars that were also jihadists, AQI sent him to Syria, where his job was to make sure that the AQI's online advertising and information was loyal to ultraconservative Islam. He was also able to help several foreign jihadists cross Syria's border in Iraq. At the time, Syrian president Bashar al-Assad was almost encouraging jihadists to go into Iraq to punish the United States for invading. By doing good work for AQI, al-Badri was building up his reputation among its top leaders. Since he was so far away from Iraq, however, he was not well known among the regular fighters.

Al-Badri was an excellent soccer player. He even impressed his fellow inmates in prison, many of whom he would convert to Islamic extremism.

Al-Badri made many connections with extremists in the American prison at Camp Bucca, shown here.

Al-Badri Rises to Power

Al-Badri joined al-Qaeda in Iraq in 2006, where he quickly won over both Abu Omar al-Baghdadi and Abu Ayyub al-Masri because of his academic credentials and the work he had done supervising religious affairs. Al-Masri named al-Badri as the supervisor of the Sharia Committee, which was responsible for enforcing ISI's strict Islamic code. He was eventually named to the Consultative Council, a group of advisors who were supposed to assist Abu Omar but really worked for al-Masri. Al-Badri was now very close to the leaders of the Islamic State; he was trusted with their secrets and plans. He was responsible for coordinating communication between those leaders and their al-Qaeda bosses. In 2010, the Iraqi government intercepted one of his letter carriers who was taking messages between Abu Omar and the ISI commander in Baghdad, al-Rawi. That captured messenger led the Iraqis right to al-Rawi,

who gave them the information they needed to eliminate Abu Omar and al-Masri.

When the top two leaders in the Islamic State were killed, al-Qaeda in Afghanistan cautioned the State not to be too quick to appoint a new leader. Bin Laden told the Consultative Council to appoint a temporary leader and to send him a list of candidates and their credentials. Growing more and more independent, the Islamic State ignored them.

A man named Hajji Bakr was head of the Islamic State's military council at the time; this made him a powerful figure when al-Masri and Abu Omar were killed. Trying to control the succession of a new leader of ISI, he wrote to each of the other members of the council claiming that everyone had agreed that Ibrahim Awwad Ibrahim al-Badri should be in charge. It is not completely clear why Bakr chose al-Badri. He may have thought al-Badri would not be as loyal to

THE ORIGINS OF
ABU BAKR AL-BAGHDADI

Al-Badri's new name was not chosen at random. Abu Bakr was the name of the Prophet Muhammad's father-in-law and the first caliph. Baghdad was the capital of the Abbasid dynasty, a great caliphate of early Islam. The Abbasids gained power in the 700s through apocalyptic propaganda and rebellion against the ruling government in Damascus; al-Baghdadi was clearly looking to mimic this tactic. The name also solidified his position as a native Iraqi.

al-Qaeda, which would have been a benefit for ISI extremism. Additionally, al-Badri had quite a few things in his favor: He had been close to the previous leader, he had powerful friends, and above all, he claimed descent from the Prophet Muhammad. Bakr believed that al-Badri could help the Islamic State make a major comeback. These efforts by Hajji Bakr were successful—al-Badri became Abu Bakr al-Baghdadi, the third leader of Iraq's growing terrorist organization. Hajji Bakr became al-Baghdadi's prime minister, and all other leaders in the State who were suspected of disloyalty were dismissed. If they did not go willingly, al-Baghdadi and Bakr had them killed.

The Resurrection of the Islamic State

Since 2007, when the Islamic State had been at its most powerful, it had taken some serious damage. The State possessed no land. It blamed this misfortune on the Americans and the Sunni tribes who had been "awakened" by General Petraeus to fight against them. With al-Baghdadi in power in 2010, the Islamic State promised itself, its remaining followers, and its enemies that it would recover.

The Islamic State's plan was not to focus on the Americans, who were on their way out. Instead, they would focus on the Iraqi military that the Americans had left with directions to keep the peace. They also planned on giving money and weapons to the Sunni tribal leaders, just as the Americans had done to create the Sons of Iraq. Since the Islamic State was now run completely by Iraqis, old grudges were being forgotten. The Islamic State wanted to instill fear in Iraq. It did this by developing a media strategy to show off its brutal methods to the public. Al-Baghdadi followed al-Zarqawi's example all too well: The Shia were still the targets, and suicide bombers were still the weapons.

Under al-Baghdadi

With al-Baghdadi's influence, the Islamic State became stronger. It grew and attracted thousands of Muslims to its cause. Every major decision and law claimed to follow the prophetic methodology, meaning that it followed the prophecy and example of Muhammad. It committed itself to purifying the world by killing anyone who opposed the absolute rule of Islam. It is hard to know how many people have been killed by ISIS, but the number is continually increasing. Most of the deaths are Muslims who oppose the ideals of ISIS. Al-Baghdadi does let Christians who do not resist live—as long as they pay a special tax called the jizya.

Many Muslim organizations have claimed that the Islamic State is un-Islamic. However, Princeton scholar Bernard Haykel says that it is not so simple. He explained that all Sunni Muslims share the texts on which ISIS bases its principles. He wrote that these texts lay out "what their religion has historically and legally required."[14] Haykel pointed out that the fighters in modern ISIS are representative of early Islamic soldiers. They are even reproducing the way Muhammad himself waged war, including slavery, crucifixion, and beheadings. According to the Koran, crucifixion is one of the only punishments permitted for anyone who stands against Islam. In addition, the jizya that al-Baghdadi has enforced against Christians is also taken directly from the Koran. Although it seems impossible to support actions such as this in the 21st century, it is important to understand that fundamentalist Muslims might support ISIS because many of its horrific actions are justifiable by certain interpretations of the Koran. It has passages that support both peace and violence.

Thousands of foreign Muslims have immigrated to the Islamic State from all over the world, including France, the United Kingdom, Belgium, Germany, Holland, Australia, Indonesia, and the United States. These men and women want to fight on the side of ISIS and are more than willing to die for their beliefs. The Internet has been an essential help in recruiting these foreign Muslims. From their homes, conservative Muslims can reach out to recruits online and arrange travel to Iraq and Syria.

Many ultraconservative Muslims consider al-Baghdadi a legitimate caliph. This means that he is a Muslim man of Qurayshi descent (meaning he is from the tribe of Muhammad), he exhibits morality, he shows a physical and mental devotion to Islam, and he has authority. Authority requires the caliph to have territory in which he can enforce Islamic law. To acquire this territory, al-Baghdadi and his followers have been making their way through as much of Syria, Iraq, and the surrounding area as they can, killing anyone who stands against them.

CHAPTER FOUR

SYRIA, MOSUL, AND THE ESTABLISHMENT OF THE CALIPHATE

Abu Bakr al-Baghdadi has taken the Islamic State under his control, and he rules with an iron fist. He is quick to punish or murder anyone who breaks any of his strict and inhumane rules and laws. From his humble beginnings as a soccer player and devout Muslim, he has turned into one of the most aggressive and violent leaders in the world. Thousands of radicals believe in his ability to lead them to paradise and believe in his observations about the end of the world. Though his ability to lead these extremists is one of his greatest talents, he has been assisted by the political unrest in many Middle Eastern countries, such as the civil war in Syria.

Because Syria, Iraq, Afghanistan, and Jordan are all clustered around each other, these countries have been used as bases of operation for terrorist groups since the rise of the original al-Qaeda in the 1980s. The Soviet invasion of Afghanistan proved that unstable lands are the perfect place for small terror organizations to grow. The same was true of the nearby country of Syria when its people rose up against an oppressive government. ISIS moved in, established a foothold, and used the war as a tool for its own advancement. These internal conflicts not only shield the jihadist groups from outsider intervention, they make it easy to take advantage of a weakened population. The Islamic State has seized these opportunities at every turn.

Syrian Unrest

According to United States intelligence reports, in 2007, nearly 90 percent of the foreign fighters that were arriving in Iraq to fight for the Islamic State were coming through Syria. Many intelligence workers and historians have wondered how that number could be so high. The reason why ISIS and other terrorist groups have been able to recruit heavily through Syria is because of that country's recent history of political unhappiness and violence. Countries plagued with violence are much easier to use for jihadist purposes, and the Syrian people's unrest toward the government began with their former president, Hafiz al-Assad, in the 1980s.

Hafiz al-Assad came to power in Syria during the 1960s and 1970s when his political party overthrew the government. After being elected president in 1971, he was quick to suppress anyone who spoke against his new government. In addition to arresting or killing political activists, al-Assad's most infamous deed was putting down a rebellion in the Syrian city of Hama in 1982. Part of this military action resulted in the massacre of 20,000 soldiers and civilians. Although this brutal suppression made al-Assad powerful, his son, who would become president of Syria in 2000, learned that his people would only tolerate that kind of oppression for a few more years.

When Bashar al-Assad succeeded his father as Syrian president, some people were optimistic that he would reform the tyrannical practices of the government. Bashar himself pledged to make his presidency less bloody and more open than his father's. For a few months after he assumed power, he kept these promises. Soon, however, he began to crack down just as violently on political activists and anyone who spoke against his policies. Many people still saw the country as an "authoritarian, totalitarian and cliquish regime."[15] Syrians endured this bad treatment for another decade.

Shortly after Abu Bakr al-Baghdadi took power in the Islamic State in 2010, Syrians were coming together to protest their current president, Bashar al-Assad. The protests started after the arrests of 15 students for painting antigovernment graffiti on the walls of a school. The community was outraged at how the children were treated. They refused to be intimidated by the police and gathered in the streets to march and demonstrate against Bashar. As his forces violently struck out against the protestors, many people, both in Syria and internationally, called for Bashar al-Assad to resign.

As unrest turned into a civil war, Syrians began demanding that Bashar give up his position. In response to these demands, Bashar released hundreds of prisoners—many of them jihadists—in order to create violence among the protestors and have a just cause for a forceful crackdown. He has consistently claimed that foreign terrorists are behind his country's civil war.

When Bashar did this, the Islamic State deployed a group to Syria to take advantage of the chaos. Al-Baghdadi sent Abu Muhammad al-Jawlani to oversee this effort and establish a branch of the Islamic State in Syria. This new group called themselves Jabhat al-Nusra, or the al-Nusra Front.

After succeeding his father, Syrian president Bashar al-Assad, pictured here, did not follow through with his promises for social reform.

Sparked by governmental violence in response to peaceful protests, the civil war in Syria has destroyed countless homes and lives.

Al-Nusra Front

In August of 2012, al-Nusra was a small jihadist group in Syria. They have grown and expanded quickly. They have taken responsibility for numerous suicide bombings throughout Syria. The group has made public statements claiming, "We are Syrian mujahideen, back from various jihad fronts to restore God's rule on the Earth and avenge the Syrians' violated honour and spilled blood. Jabhat al-Nusra has taken upon itself to be the Muslim nation's weapon in this land."[16] Al-Nusra means "support" in Arabic, and it has gained a reputation for honesty and trying to appeal to ordinary Muslims.

The call for support stopped many of the group's suicide attacks, and it started collaborating with other Sunni groups. Claiming to support Syrian rebels, al-Nusra aimed its attacks at the government militia and police forces. However, it is still a product of the Islamic State, acknowledging the United States and Israel as enemies of Islam. It has also attacked other religious groups in Syria, including the Alawites, which is a Shiite sect. President Bashar al-Assad is an Alawite.

The al-Nusra Front created its own flag, separate from the Islamic State's. The two groups have clashed over tactical and religious choices.

Despite being formed by the Islamic State, al-Nusra does not operate as its parent organization does. The Islamic State practices unlimited dictatorial power, while al-Nusra shares power and collaborates with other organizations. This has caused ISIS to disagree and fight with its Syrian branch. The Islamic State is also envious of the land that al-Nusra is able to control. An American journalist, Theo Padnos, was held as an al-Nusra hostage from 2012 to 2014. He claimed, "the real issue between the Nusra Front and the Islamic State was that their commanders, former friends from Iraq, were unable to agree on how to share the revenue from the oil fields in eastern Syria that the Nusra Front had conquered."[17]

The Islamic State Versus al-Nusra Front

Soon, Abu Bakr al-Baghdadi began to suspect that the fighters in Syria under al-Nusra were more loyal to their leader, al-Jawlani, than they were to him, the commander of the faithful. Al-Baghdadi then instructed al-Jawlani to make it clear to al-Nusra fighters that they were members of the Islamic State. Al-Jawlani refused. He insisted that al-Nusra existed in Syria at the request of al-Qaeda and they would not answer to the Islamic State.

Despite this, al-Nusra did not want to publicly declare its association with al-Qaeda, either. Being openly associated with a terrorist organization would destroy the support it had worked to build. Al-Baghdadi took initiative in April 2013 to claim al-Nusra as Islamic State property, despite al-Jawlani's resistance. He declared that al-Nusra would be absorbed into a new organization: the Islamic State of Iraq and al-Sham, or the Islamic State of Iraq and Syria—ISIS.

However, al-Jawlani was not going to accept al-Baghdadi's bullying. He quickly declared independence from the Islamic State and publicly pledged allegiance to al-Qaeda and Ayman al-Zawahiri, its leader. In response, al-Qaeda scolded both men for the needless arguing and told the Islamic State to stay within Iraq while al-Nusra would continue to fight in Syria under al-Qaeda. Al-Baghdadi quickly rejected this decision. Al-Qaeda's effort to contain the Islamic State by national borders only made al-Baghdadi and his State more sure of their right to be in Syria. In early 2014, al-Qaeda publicly renounced any connection to the Islamic State.

The relations between the two terrorist organizations were poor. Abu Khalid, the man chosen by al-Qaeda to help the situation between al-Nusra and the Islamic State, was disgusted. He said, "the State group is excommunicating everyone who opposes them or differs with them, spilling their blood with [no punishment] as if they own Islam."[18] In response, the Islamic State threatened to send five suicide bombers to murder Khalid; later, it followed through with that threat. After Khalid's death, the rebellion against the Islamic State weakened and eventually fell. Thousands of jihadists left al-Nusra to officially join ISIS. Eventually, the group was renamed Jabhat Fateh al-Sham and cut ties with both the Islamic State and al-Qaeda.

U.S. Involvement

Abu Bakr al-Baghdadi constantly worked to rebuild the Islamic State, helping fuel the civil war in Syria. Tactics such as car bombings had worked for him in Iraq, and they worked equally well in Syria. As casualties grew and innocent people were fleeing the country, the United States decided it needed to get involved. President Obama was reluctant; he did not want to get further involved in the violence of the Middle East. However, his advisors insisted that they needed to give those fighting back against al-Baghdadi the weapons to succeed in that fight. It took about a year for Obama to authorize any kind of assistance, but the government eventually shipped light weapons to the Syrian rebels. By that time, however, it was too late; al-Baghdadi's military force was too strong. Despite the growing threat, President Obama continued to resist authorizing U.S. military intervention. ISIS still was not seen as an equivalent to al-Qaeda in terms of the danger it posed to American citizens.

ISIS captured the city of Mosul in northern Iraq almost overnight. This was a major victory for the jihadists and a major blow to the Iraqi government.

Taking Mosul

Al-Baghdadi entered Syria and quickly set up the ISIS headquarters in the northern city of Raqqa. However, with the leader of ISIS gone, the Iraqi government started to crack down on the Sunni population. Prime Minister Nouri al-Maliki took the opportunity of al-Baghdadi's absence to try to suppress any resistance by the Sunnis.

Near the start of 2014, al-Baghdadi turned his attention back to his home country. Many oppressed Sunnis were eager to join his terrorist group—not necessarily because they were jihadists, but because they wanted to end the tyranny of al-Maliki. These new recruits allowed ISIS to keep a strong presence in Syria while simultaneously conquering Iraqi cities. Their most important

capture was the city of Mosul, Iraq's second-largest population center. ISIS fighters easily took the western bank of the city, causing Iraqi government soldiers and police officers to abandon their posts while thousands of Iraqi civilians fled. This greatly exposed the weakness of Iraq's security forces, and ISIS was able to capture an arsenal of weapons and military equipment.

Mosul was a significant win for al-Baghdadi. It is located in a strategically important intersection, linking Iraq to Turkey and Syria. Prime Minister al-Maliki declared a state of emergency and claimed that his government would not let Mosul fall "under the shadow of terror and terrorists,"[19] but it seemed impossible to reclaim the city. Capturing Mosul put ISIS on the map, demonstrating to both its followers and its enemies that it was more powerful than many had thought. It was capable of quickly taking command of a geographically important piece of land.

Al-Baghdadi's Sermon

On July 4, 2014, al-Baghdadi publicly broadcasted himself for the first time. In a sermon at a mosque in Mosul that he recorded and published online, he declared himself the ruler of the global caliphate—the leader of Muslims worldwide—and called on his subjects to carry out the holy war against those he considers infidels: "God created us to worship him and spread his religion, and ordered us to fight his enemies for him and for religion."[20]

Al-Baghdadi's sermon was a surprise for those at the mosque. According to a witness, black vehicles with tinted windows pulled up, and men got out chanting "*Allahu akbar*," which means "Allah is great." Those in the mosque were then told that al-Baghdadi would give a sermon and they must listen. Jihadists who came in with al-Baghdadi took over the first row, and their faces were blurred before the video was distributed. Then civilians in the mosque were kept prisoner for an hour. Gunmen were posted at the doors to block any exit. This sermon symbolized that al-Baghdadi had finally turned Abu Musab al-Zarqawi's vision into a reality. The Islamic State was going global.

Al-Baghdadi specifically copied the ancient Abbasid caliphs of Islam during his sermon. He wore black robes in their honor and even paraphrased what the first caliph, from whom he took his name, said when he was elected by Muhammad's followers: "I was appointed to rule you, but I am not the best among you. If you see me acting truly, then follow me. If you see me acting falsely, then advise and guide me … If I disobey God, then do not obey me."[21] Regardless of his words, it was obvious that everyone was expected to obey the new caliph.

After the Islamic State seized Mosul in June 2014, al-Baghdadi and ISIS ruled an area larger than the size of the United Kingdom. While bin Laden and al-Qaeda did not expect to see a true caliphate in their lifetime, al-Baghdadi and his Islamic State required and obtained united and structured territory. A caliphate had not been functional in any real way for about 1,000 years. Al-Baghdadi's sermon brought thousands of jihadists to Syria daily, all of whom were "ready to give up everything at home for a shot at paradise."[22] Declaring a caliphate meant that all Muslims were required to immigrate to the territory where the caliph was applying his laws. By reminding people of the Mahdi, Islam's mystical savior, and predicting the apocalypse, ISIS used fear to help their recruiting efforts. According to their interpretation of the Koran, all Muslims must be within the caliphate when the armies of the West collide with the armies of Islam in the northern Syrian city of Dabiq.

A Time for Action

Once the Islamic State took Mosul, the previously reluctant U.S. government had to take action. American planes began bombing runs soon after. In response, ISIS murdered its American and European prisoners. In order to mimic the Iraqi prisoners in American custody, the victims were dressed in orange jumpsuits.

After the sermon at Mosul, the media reported al-Baghdadi dead or wounded twice, in November 2014 and March 2015, but he issued public statements assuring his fighters he was alive and well. Officials have questioned what will happen after al-Baghdadi. Some argued that when (and if) he died, he would just be replaced with another jihadist. However, the *New York Times* reported that al-Baghdadi himself made arrangements in case of his death by splitting up his military powers among his subordinates. In any case, few of his followers have the same credentials as Abu Bakr al-Baghdadi. He claims origins from Prophet Muhammad, has a doctoral degree in Koranic studies, and has led ISIS to the gains it has had from 2011 to 2016 and beyond.

THE CALIPHATE AND THE COMING APOCALYPSE

When Abu Bakr al-Baghdadi declared that he was the caliph of a new, worldwide Muslim society, it was a major turning point for the events of the Middle East. Islamic believers who were already radical saw it as a call to arms; thousands of people came to Syria and Iraq to join ISIS and fight for the caliph. Millions more Muslims condemned this declaration and al-Baghdadi's terrorist actions. Governments from across the world began to take this organization much more seriously. The focus shifted from al-Qaeda to the Islamic State.

As of 2016, despite the best efforts of the United States and other countries, ISIS has been able to acquire and hold a huge area of land. Between the national boundaries between Iraq and Syria, the Islamic State has claimed a large amount of land, which is occupied by a large number of people. Though few of the inhabitants of the lands they have conquered are supporters of ISIS, they are still forced to live under extremist rule. If they do not, they are killed. Moreover, the recruiters for ISIS are slowly working on turning normal Muslims into mindless soldiers who will fight and kill for their radical purposes. One of the ways they are doing this is by predicting the apocalypse.

The Apocalypse

Islamic ideas of the end of the world are very similar in nature to any that exist in other major religions, such as Judaism or Christianity. Their largely common belief is that some time in the future, God will pass judgment on all who are still on Earth, with some going to heaven and some going to hell, and the world will end. However, the Koran itself does not include an explicit portion about the apocalypse. Because of this, Muslim beliefs regarding the apocalypse come from supplementary material, such as the other writings of the Prophet Muhammad and the Bible.

An expert on Islamic theology, David Cook, explained that events surrounding the Islamic end of the world are broken into two groups: the Lesser Signs of the Hour and the Greater Signs of the Hour. The Lesser Signs are "moral, cultural, political, religious, and natural events designed to warn humanity that the end is near and to bring people into a state of repentance."[23] These signs are generic and could be found anywhere in history. The Greater Signs, however, are a much more detailed account of what Muslims should expect in the final days on Earth: Modern-day Istanbul will be conquered by Muslims, the Antichrist will travel to Jerusalem and the Mahdi (or Jesus, in some interpretations) will kill him, everyone will be converted to Islam, and all infidel territories will be dominated.

Years before the Islamic State, al-Qaeda had been using the apocalypse as a tool. Most of their claims, however, were more symbolic than literal. They claimed that the Mahdi would appear in an area called Khorasan, which includes parts of Iran, Central Asia, and Afghanistan, with an army carrying black flags supporting him. The Islamic State, however, took the prophecy of the apocalypse literally; it is here that the Syrian city of Dabiq takes on an important role.

The Battle in Dabiq

The tiny, north-Syrian city Dabiq is crucial for the future the Islamic State imagines for itself. When Abu Musab al-Zarqawi began the organization that became known as the Islamic State, he said, "The spark has been lit here in Iraq, and its heat will continue to intensify … until it burns the crusader armies in Dabiq."[24] From the very beginning of his terrorist career, al-Zarqawi and his followers preached about the end of the world. Islamic apocalypse prophecies often refer to these "crusader armies" as Rome, but it is doubtful that they mean the capital city of Italy. Some think references to Rome mean the Eastern Roman Empire, which had its capital in what is now Istanbul, Turkey. Other Muslim sources say that Rome could mean any army of infidels, such as the Americans.

The Islamic State captured Dabiq in the summer of 2014. Soon afterward, it released the first issue of an English-language magazine, also named *Dabiq*. As an area of great importance leading up to the end of the world, ISIS believed it was necessary to raise the black flags of the caliphate and cleanse the city of sin. In November 2014, ISIS released a video online announcing it had killed a young aid worker and former United States Army Ranger named Abdul-Rahman Kassig. The executioner claimed Kassig had been killed at Dabiq, saying, "Here we are, burying the first American Crusader in Dabiq, eagerly waiting for the

The small city of Dabiq is a large piece in ISIS's propaganda. They believe that a final, apocalyptic battle will occur there.

remainder of your armies to arrive."[25] Many Islamic State followers saw this murder as the beginning of the apocalyptic battle.

The Islamic State believes that a battle in Dabiq will be fought, and they will win it. Afterward, many believe that the caliphate will take over the entire planet. According to the apocalyptic literature, an Antichrist named Dajjal will come from eastern Iran and kill almost all of the caliphate's fighters. The survivors will supposedly be forced to retreat to Jerusalem. Then, ISIS believes, Jesus will return to earth, kill Dajjal, and lead the Muslims to victory.

Attracting the Masses

The more enemies who consider intervening and attacking the Islamic State in Dabiq, the more excited the jihadists get about the prophecy of the battle. When the United States began considering military action against the Islamic State in Syria, one jihadist tweeted, "Thirty states remain to complete the number of eighty flags that will gather in Dabiq and begin the battle."[26] Promising the end of the world is one of the most powerful ways that al-Baghdadi and ISIS recruit new extremists. By explicitly claiming that the world is about to end, the group is implying that any Muslim who does not help them will be condemned to hell—and any who assist them will be promised a heavenly paradise. The jihadists believe that their responsibility is to gather in Syria and be prepared to fight for the cause of an Islamic apocalypse.

Foreign extremists who travel to fight in distant countries call themselves strangers because they adhere to the "true Islam" they think most Muslims ignore or neglect. The strangers have abandoned their home countries to fight the final battle against the infidels and never expect to return alive. One fighter from northern Syria boasted, "We have here the mujahideen from Russia, America, the Philippines, China, Germany, Belgium, Sudan, India and Yemen and other places. They are here because this [is] what the Prophet said and promised, the Grand Battle is happening."[27]

The *New York Times* interviewed many young Tunisians who aligned themselves with the Islamic State's foreign fighters. Tunisians make up a large number of those pledged to ISIS. The coming apocalypse is part of what attracts these young men to the organization. A 24-year-old said, "There are lots of signs that the end will be soon, according to the [Koran]."[28] However, the Koran itself says little about the apocalypse. Further, almost none of these young Tunisians believe that the Islamic State has been involved in mass killings or beheadings. They think these violent actions are rumors being spread by the West. These young jihadists complain that no one in the Arab government is a pure scholar of Islam, that they are all corrupted by power, and that this in itself could be another sign that the world is coming to an end.

Extremists from all over the world are attracted to the Islamic State's principles. Thousands have immigrated to the Islamic State and defend it with their lives.

Plenty of Prophecies

In Islamic apocalypse texts, the important figure of the Antichrist is described in detail. Commonly, he is an ugly, one-eyed creature who has one hand longer than the other. One part of the prophecy is repeatedly and conveniently ignored, however: It is written that this Dajjal will first appear in the area between Syria and Iraq—which is exactly where the Islamic State is located.

These prophecies are biased because they were written during similar religious conflicts that occurred centuries ago in Iraq and Syria. Prophecies predict the coming of the Sufyani, a descendant of Abu Sufyan, a man who prosecuted the Prophet Muhammad. The Shia believe the Sufyani will fight the imam (leader of a Muslim community) and the Prophet will kill him, while the Sunnis believe the Sufyani will reconcile with the Mahdi and restore the caliphate to him. The Sufyani symbolizes a period of fighting between Muslim communities before the final judgment day.

One prophecy claims that when black and yellow banners fight in Syria, the land will be destroyed. The Islamic

Members of ISIS believe that the yellow flags of Hezbollah are yet another symbol of the coming end of the world.

State's flag is infamously black, and they believe that the yellow banners stand for the Hezbollah, a Shia military organization. The word Hezbollah means party of God, but the jihadists call it Hizb al Shaytan, which means the party of Satan. The organization holds a lot of power in Lebanon, but it has been accused of committing violence against Israel and is widely considered a terrorist organization. When the war in Syria started, thousands of Hezbollah fighters went to fight for Syrian president Bashar al-Assad. This made them enemies of Sunni militants and the Islamic State.

The Emergence of Sharia Law

Followers of the Islamic State celebrate every major step toward the return of Islamic law. In 2014, the State reinstated the acceptance of slavery, especially of women. Although Muslim countries abolished slavery in the 19th century, the Koran allows it. Al-Qaeda never revived slavery, but the Islamic State does so publicly. A spokesperson of ISIS has promised: "We will conquer your Rome, break your crosses, and enslave your women … If we do not reach that time, then our children and grandchildren will reach it, and they will sell your sons as slaves at the slave market."[29] In October 2014, the Islamic State declared that female children, ages 1 to 9, would be worth 200,000 Iraqi dinars (about $170) and 50,000 dinars (about $40) less for each additional decade of age.

In 2016, a UN report estimated that ISIS held 3,500 people as slaves. Most of these slaves were women and children from the Yazidi community. Yazidism is an ancient religion whose roughly 1 million followers live primarily in Iraq. The religion takes pieces from Christianity, Islam, and Judaism, yet believers are unjustly considered devil-worshippers by some and have suffered from persecution for centuries. They are largely Kurds, a people mostly closely related to Iranians, and they are a minority in Iraq. Al-Qaeda and ISIS declared Yazidis infidels and allowed their fighters to kill them indiscriminately. The enslavement of the Yazidis stems from religious and cultural intolerance. Moreover, the emergence of the slave trade is another sign, for radical Muslims, that the apocalypse is near.

There are many Yazidi refugees running from the violence of the Islamic State. Those who cannot escape are enslaved or murdered.

A Self-Made Caliphate

To his followers, the caliph represents political and spiritual power. Sunnis felt that the abolition of the last caliphate after World War I was the end of Muslim political power and a big victory for the West. The main goal of modern jihadists is to fight to restore the caliphate. Most, including Osama bin Laden, saw it as a distant goal. By declaring a caliphate, Abu Bakr al-Baghdadi and the Islamic State demonstrated that popular opinion could be ignored and the West does not have to be feared. Al-Baghdadi took some land, declared it his own, and proved to many jihadists that the goal was not so distant. When the caliphate was announced, one jihadist tweeted, "the Islamic State has no borders, and its conquests will continue, with God's permission."[30]

After al-Baghdadi declared the caliphate, billboards appeared across Iraq and Syria reading, "No god but God" and "The Islamic State: A Caliphate in Accordance with the Prophetic Method." These phrases were also put on coins minted by the Islamic State, which were created to sever ties to the current government. Despite its popularity, not all jihadists believe that the Islamic State is the true caliphate. Some believe the claim is illegitimate because a majority of Muslim leaders do not endorse it. The only people in power who claimed al-Baghdadi as the caliph were the senior leaders of the Islamic State itself. As for al-Qaeda, instead of denying al-Baghdadi, its leaders have hinted that the head of the Taliban is the true caliph.

Despite this, the Islamic State and its self-proclaimed caliphate sparked a spirit of loyalty around the world. A young Tunisian jihadist wrote, "To all my brothers in Tunisia who have Jihad in their hearts, the Caliphate has been established … it is a great blessing."[31]

CHAPTER SIX

THE IMPACT OF
ISIS

By predicting the end of the world and bringing up ancient prophecies, the Islamic State is recruiting extremists who will be loyal to its cause. They believe that they will be sent to heaven, even if they die fighting for a terrorist cause, and that every person they murder is an infidel who deserved to die for not following Abu Bakr al-Baghdadi. Though military resistance in 2016 has reduced the size of al-Baghdadi's caliphate, its fighters are still committing violence in the name of religion. They are not only destroying countless lives, they are taking a toll on the entire Middle East.

Because its leaders believe that Allah has given them orders to murder and spread their radical Islam, ISIS has no fear and no boundaries. It has recruited young children to fight for it, employed hundreds of suicide bombers, and destroyed countless cultural artifacts.

Abu Bakr al-Baghdadi has turned the small organization of amateur terrorists into a major military force in the Middle East. ISIS has become wealthy and powerful under his rule, and that has had horrible consequences for the entire world.

Who Fights for ISIS?

In 2011, a teenage Muslim named Abdelaziz Kuwan from the island country of Bahrain decided to defy his family's wishes and travel to Syria to fight for al-Nusra. There, he earned a reputation for being brave, ruthless, and very dedicated to the Islamic cause. At the end of 2012, he returned home to Bahrain and the family he left there but found that his former life had nothing for him anymore: "I walk in the streets and I feel imprisoned. I feel tied up. It's like someone is always watching me. This world means nothing to me. I want to be free. I want to go back. People are giving their lives. That's the honorable life."[32]

Kuwan did go back—and this time joined the Islamic State. His violence and cruelty were considered valuable attributes, and he was eventually appointed as a security official. In October 2014, he was shot and killed. Jihadists generally write a will before they fight, and his was addressed to his mother:

> As you know and watch on television channels, the infidels … have gone too far in their oppression, killing, torture, and violations of Muslims' honor. I, by God, cannot see my Muslim sisters and brothers being killed … and I sit without doing anything … I longed for heaven, near the Prophet Muhammad.[33]

Kuwan's life and death are tragic examples of many young Muslim men who put their faith in the Islamic State. They not only willingly volunteer, but they feel a serious responsibility to dedicate their time and lives to radical Islam. Women also join the Islamic State; they may not fight, but they work toward serving the men. One group of women, called the Khansa Brigade, polices the female slaves. The caliphate promises honor and eternal glory to Islamic youth who may feel isolated from their home societies and communities. The immigrants into Syria have been traveling to the caliphate on one-way tickets. Some have been captured on video burning their European or Australian passports. Those who cannot immigrate for various reasons have become very frustrated and, sometimes, attacked targets in the West.

Even though the Islamic State has adequately demonstrated that it does not care about its public reputation, it has attempted to show that it cares about those jihadists who pledge allegiance to its organization; it has recorded videos of food being handed out to those in need and general humanitarian relief. These small efforts, however, are more like propaganda—the quality of life for everyone in Iraq and Syria has greatly diminished.

Guidelines for the Caliphate

It is not just the people of the caliphate who have to follow strict rules. As a territory and institution, it also has to follow regulations set by the prophecies of Islam. An essential duty of the caliph is to continue to wage war and expand the caliphate. Foreign policy such as this is called offensive jihad: the forcible expansion into non-Muslim countries. The prophecy requires the eventual conquest of every country on Earth. In *Dabiq*, an author wrote, "The shade of [ISIS's] flag will expand until it covers all eastern and western extents of the Earth, filling the world with the truth and justice of Islam and putting an end to the falsehood and tyranny."[34]

While the caliphate is required to gain land, Islamic law does permit temporary peace treaties with other nations. These treaties can last no longer than a decade. They are renewable but cannot be applied to all enemies at once. In addition, the caliph and his followers must commit at least one major jihadist action every year.

Unlike al-Qaeda, which can exist underground and in secret, if the Islamic State loses its grip on the territory it won in Syria and Iraq, it is not likely to survive. Caliphates must have authority over land; if ISIS does not, all the oaths of allegiance from the young Muslim jihadists are no longer sacred. The Islamic State claims that there is a religious duty to immigrate to and fight for the State—if their territory disappears, so does that obligation. This makes it important for the Islamic State to acquire, and not lose, land.

With every month that ISIS fails to expand its geographic territory, the less it resembles a conquering state and the more it appears to be a small, failing Middle Eastern government. Combat efforts from the non-Sunni Muslims, mainly the Shia and the Kurds, are the best chance for the Islamic State to be destroyed. If the United States were to bring military activity to the region again, it would only confirm the suspicions of the Islamic State that the West wants to kill Muslims. This would ultimately improve recruitment of jihadists.

SHARIA PUNISHMENTS

Where the Islamic State moved in, communities suffered. Those groups who cooperated and handed over their territory willingly were given some money and basic necessities. Anyone who did not cooperate was eliminated or kidnapped. The Islamic State enforced *hudud* punishments, which are specific penalties described directly in the Koran. These included death for speaking against Islam, homosexual acts, treason, and murder; death by stoning for those who committed adultery; and amputation of a hand for stealing. The State carried out these sentences publicly and forced crowds of civilians to watch to terrify everyone into submission. Even something as simple as smoking cigarettes was punishable by whipping, severing fingers, or jail time. No one was safe or above the sharia law—even Islamic State commanders were punished according to their crime.

How Does ISIS Fund Its Terror?

It is important to know how an institution such as the Islamic State makes money. Any self-governing territory needs money—even one whose leaders claim it is blessed by God. The

Islamic State frequently profits from ransoming kidnapped foreigners. It is following al-Qaeda in this regard. The United States Treasury estimated that between 2004 and 2012, al-Qaeda made $120 million from paid ransoms. In 2013 alone, al-Qaeda made $66 million. The Islamic State has used them as an example.

The United States has a general policy of refusing to pay ransoms, but executions of Western hostages have caused debate over whether those policies need to be changed. ISIS kidnapped James Foley, an American journalist, in 2012 in northwestern Syria. Foley was then ransomed to the American government for hundreds of millions of dollars. When the United States would not agree to the ransom, the Islamic Sate executed him on camera and released the video publicly.

Aside from brutal terror tactics, ISIS makes money in some more conventional ways. Its territory is "taxed." This means that citizens must pay to survive, and businesses are taxed for electricity and security. Checkpoints are set up throughout Iraq and Syria, and drivers who wish to go through must pay a toll, which is a fee for using the road.

Most wealth-generating tactics of the Islamic State are illegal, however, such as when members raided several Mosul banks in June 2014 and stole an estimated $500 million.

The biggest geographical advantage the Islamic State has is the natural oil it sits on. ISIS makes $1 million to $2 million every day from selling oil to the rest of the world. The oil

There are major oil reserves beneath the feet of ISIS fighters in Iraq and Syria. Stations similar to this one have been major sources of income for terrorists.

comes from refineries and wells that are found in Islamic State territory in northern Iraq and Syria. This oil is smuggled into southern Turkey and sold.

The United States has repeatedly targeted the Islamic State's oil assets. It is not good for the rest of the world that the caliphate is self-sustaining from a natural resource. It produces about 44,000 barrels of oil a day in Syria and about 4,000 barrels a day in Iraq.

Selling the Past

The Islamic State is located in an area that not only has a lot of oil, but also a lot of history. The Middle East is rich in ancient archeological sites that contain old and valuable pieces of art and architecture. ISIS allows local citizens to dig in the ancient sites that it controls, as long as the State is given a certain percentage of the value of whatever is found. ISIS goes as far as to encourage field crews to dig in some parts of the area surrounding the Euphrates River in hopes that a valuable discovery will be made.

The Islamic State has caused massive and permanent damage to Syria's cultural history through these methods. Not only has it sold the country's heritage off to the highest bidders, but it has also used ancient historical sites, such as the third-century city of Hatra, as a training ground for recruits and a place to murder prisoners.

The Destruction of Nimrud

Not all of the Islamic State's cultural destruction is for profit, however. In March 2015, ISIS posted a video online showing a group of soldiers destroying the archaeological site in the Iraqi city of Nimrud. This city had an archaeological history of 3,000 years, and before its destruction, the government

of Iraq nominated it to be included on the United Nations Educational, Scientific, and Cultural Organization's (UNESCO) list of world heritage sites. Regardless, ISIS used sledgehammers, power tools, and explosives to destroy the cultural artifacts found there. The UN stated that the major, deliberate cultural destruction was a serious war crime. In a video of the demolition, Islamic State fighters were proud of the damage.

In another online video, ISIS supporters demolished artifacts at a museum in Mosul. In the video, a jihadist said, "These antiquities and idols behind me were from people in past centuries and

Some antiquities from Nimrud were saved before ISIS got the chance to destroy them, such as these statues of human-headed winged lions dating back to 860 BC.

were worshiped instead of God. When God Almighty orders us to destroy these statues, idols and antiquities, we must do it, even if they're worth billions of dollars."[35] He explained that not even money is as important to the Islamic State as maintaining closeness to Allah. The fact that Western viewers are disgusted by this destruction is just an added bonus.

It was clear from these and other public videos that ISIS wants to destroy the real history of Iraq and Syria permanently. Nimrud contained many frescoes (watercolor paintings done on walls and ceilings) and works of literature that had survived for

centuries. The site was so large that portions of it had not even been fully explored—and it is now likely that they never will be.

Destroying History

Nimrud is not the only ancient site that has been targeted for these reasons. Khorsabad, the capital of ancient Assyria, was destroyed in March 2015. It was the location of a palace built between 717 and 706 BC, which the Oriental Institute said exhibited "stylistic innovations, preservation of paint ... and the extensive ancient written documentation concerning the organization of the building project."[36] Now, all of these invaluable aspects of Middle Eastern history are lost. ISIS has also burned thousands of books and rare texts in the Mosul Library, in what UNESCO said is "one of the most devastating acts of destruction of library collections in human history."[37]

In July 2014, the Islamic State released a video showing the destruction of Jonah's tomb in Mosul. Jonah was a prophet and a major figure in the Islamic, Jewish, and Christian traditions. According to scriptures in all three religions, Jonah was swallowed by a whale after a shipwreck. After praying to God to save him, the whale threw Jonah up onto dry land. The Islamic State wanted to publicly destroy the tomb of Jonah because this story is a major fixture in Christian traditions. It disregarded that Jonah is also a prominent figure of Islam. The destruction of the tomb was meant to be a symbolic attack on Christians living in Iraq and on the Christian heritage of the Middle East.

The Islamic State considers all religious shrines to be insulting to Allah. Sturt W. Manning, an archaeologist from Cornell University, explained that ISIS

> is destroying the evidence of the great history of Iraq; it has to, as this history [describes] a rich alternative to its barbaric [actions]. Worse, these acts of destruction supposedly in the name of religion are dishonest and hypocritical: the same ISIS also is busy looting archaeological sites to support its thriving illegal trade in antiquities, causing further [serious] harm.[38]

The Islamic State is focused on destroying any evidence that there is another way to practice Islam—through peace and appreciation of culture—as opposed to violence and destruction. Manning also brought attention to the fact that ISIS appreciates valuable artifacts and antiques if they need the money they can bring in.

A Country Destroyed by Prejudice

There have been countless demonstrations that the Islamic State feels no responsibility to its own people. It is entirely based on prejudice, hate, and intolerance against other cultures and even against other Muslims. Although the Shia are the main targets of this hatred and have suffered greatly because of it, Sunnis have become victims as well.

The exact number of Sunnis who have been killed by anti–Islamic State fighters is unknown. However, anti-ISIS fighters may be just as violent and brutal as the group they are fighting against. Some humanitarian organizations have estimated that, in certain areas, the Islamic State is no more violent and lethal than its opposition.

The fates of Sunni refugees (Sunnis who have been forced to leave their homes to escape persecution) has been related to how successful the Islamic State has been in their terrorist activities. When ISIS took over Mosul in 2014, Sunnis were targeted outside of Baghdad. They were kidnapped or killed by Shia who were angry over ISIS's actions. Similarly, after the fall of another major city, hundreds more Sunnis were tormented by the anti-ISIS militias.

Since 2013, Sunnis have divided into three different groups: Some have joined the Islamic State, some have established Sunni militias and worked with the Iraqi government security forces, and others have fled entirely to Kurdistan or Jordan. Regardless, what remains true is that, in reality, a tiny minority of Sunnis are enemies of Shia, just as only a tiny minority of Sunnis are part of ISIS. A Sunni construction worker who escaped from the Islamic

State–controlled city of Fallujah in Iraq said, "I don't ever want to go back. Even if ISIS falls, everyone is trying to get out, get as far away from Iraq as possible."[39]

Why Is ISIS Making Enemies?

One of the biggest mysteries surrounding the Islamic State is why they are enthusiastic about making enemies. Every person murdered or enslaved and every important piece of ancient history destroyed or sold creates an enemy against ISIS. The Islamic State has made enemies of the Shia, Kurds, Yazidis, Christians, Muslims, and even its former parent group, al-Qaeda. It has united almost every nearby ethnic and religious group against it. Countries across the world, such as the United States and the entire continent of Europe, oppose the State passionately. This is all because ISIS is almost eager to gain opponents. Even Nazi Germany, which executed millions of people, tried to hide its terrible crimes from the rest of the world. By comparison, the Islamic State advertises its crimes openly, proudly, and globally on social media.

What the rest of the world thinks about it is very clear to the Islamic State. When ISIS beheaded the American journalist James Foley in 2014, the United States led a series of air

DESTROYING EACH OTHER

In late 2015, the Islamic State seized a village in the Anbar province of Iraq. Houses were blown up, and civilians were executed. One family, the Sabar family, was among those who escaped. Anbar province is the heartland of Sunni Iraq, and the Sabar family belonged to that sect. Only a few hundred families escaped the takeover, and they fled all over Iraq. The Sabar family ended up in Baghdad, the capital of Iraq and a city controlled by anti-ISIS forces.

The journey to Baghdad was difficult. They had to travel on foot through a desert filled with ISIS fighters and supporters. The Sabars did not arrive in Baghdad for more than two months. Because Baghdad was a hub of opposition to the Islamic State, the Sabars saw it as a symbol of safety. However, because the Islamic State comprises mostly extremist Sunnis, the new Shiite neighbors of the Sabars blamed them for what ISIS had done. Many Sunnis were considered part of the ISIS problem, even though they had lost everything because of them.

Like many Sunnis, the community threatened them. After a particularly bad threat, one night, the family decided to flee. Before they could escape, men came into their house with guns and accused the family of being ISIS supporters. All the grown men in the house—two brothers and a few of their adult sons—were taken. Seven of them were shot and killed for no other reason than being Sunni in Baghdad.

strikes that killed thousands of Islamic State fighters. When ISIS burned Jordanian pilot Muath al-Kaseasbeh alive in 2015, Jordan joined the American campaign against the Islamic State. Jordan is where Abu Musab al-Zarqawi, the founder of the group that evolved into ISIS, was born. When ISIS beheaded 21 Egyptians in Libya, Egypt responded by dropping bombs on Libyan Islamic State locations. Most of the world is unified in standing against this terrorist organization.

In the Name of the Apocalypse

The difference between the Islamic State and other terrorist groups is that it does not worry about its public image. Even the notorious Osama bin Laden and al-Qaeda condemned the actions of ISIS, and especially its violence against other Muslims. Groups such as ISIS, which call for the apocalypse, are the most likely to use weapons of mass destruction. Their actions are harder to predict, because their mindset is so radical.

The Islamic State does not act rationally. It does not care about making enemies because every action it carries out is supposed to bring the end of the world. ISIS believes that, as the final battle in Dabiq comes closer, there are only two options: Support the Islamic State and reach heaven, or support its opposition and be condemned to hell. The Islamic State believes that it is fighting a righteous religious war—a war that Allah has already determined it will win.

The goal of ISIS is to purify the world and start from scratch with Islam. However, it is important to remember that the Islam they want to institute is not the same religion that nearly all Muslims practice. They take advantage of sadness and fear, combining them with their radical and extreme thoughts, and kill anyone in their way.

ISIS WORLDWIDE

The Islamic State is a powerful institution that is a lethal reminder of what can happen when civil unrest and religious extremism reach their climax at the exact same time. From small, humble origins as an outpost of al-Qaeda, it has evolved into one of the most dangerous organizations in the world. Its ability to commit terrible acts of violence with great enthusiasm in the name of religion makes it a threat to anyone, in any country, or of any race. However, it is also important to remember that ISIS comprises just a small fraction of Muslims. As of 2016, fewer and fewer people were rallying around the cause of radical Islam, which is a positive turn. Nevertheless, ISIS fighters continue their reign of terror both locally and globally.

Terrorist attacks are incredibly dangerous and difficult to prevent. Extremists tend to target crowded places, where their weapons can do the most damage. They also prefer targeting people who are completely innocent. From the September 11, 2001, attacks in America to the Bastille Day 2016 strike in France, terrorism is almost always focused on causing as much damage and loss of life as possible. ISIS is currently the most powerful of radical terrorist organization, and it has done a huge amount of damage to the world.

Terror Attacks on the Western World

There have been many attacks made on the Western world by extremist Muslims in the name of the Islamic State. Hundreds of innocent people have died for no reason other than religious belief. Every attack is a reminder that the actions of the Islamic State are far-reaching and cannot be ignored just because it is geographically distant from the United States and Europe. ISIS aims to spread fear and threaten the freedom of the entire world.

On November 13, 2015, a series of coordinated attacks in Paris, France, killed 130 people and wounded hundreds more. The Islamic State targeted people at dinner, enjoying a concert, and viewing a soccer game. On March 22, 2016, attacks on an airport and a subway station in Brussels, Belgium, killed at least 30 people and wounded more than 200. The Islamic State took responsibility. On June 12, 2016, 49 people were killed in the worst mass shooting in U.S. history at a nightclub in Orlando, Florida. The man responsible called the police during his attack and pledged allegiance to ISIS.

On July 14, 2016, Mohamed Lahouaiej Bouhlel, in the name of ISIS, drove a truck into a crowd of people in Nice, France, during a fireworks show. He killed 84 people and injured more than 300. It is reported that more than one-third of the people he killed were Muslim. A spokeswoman for the Union

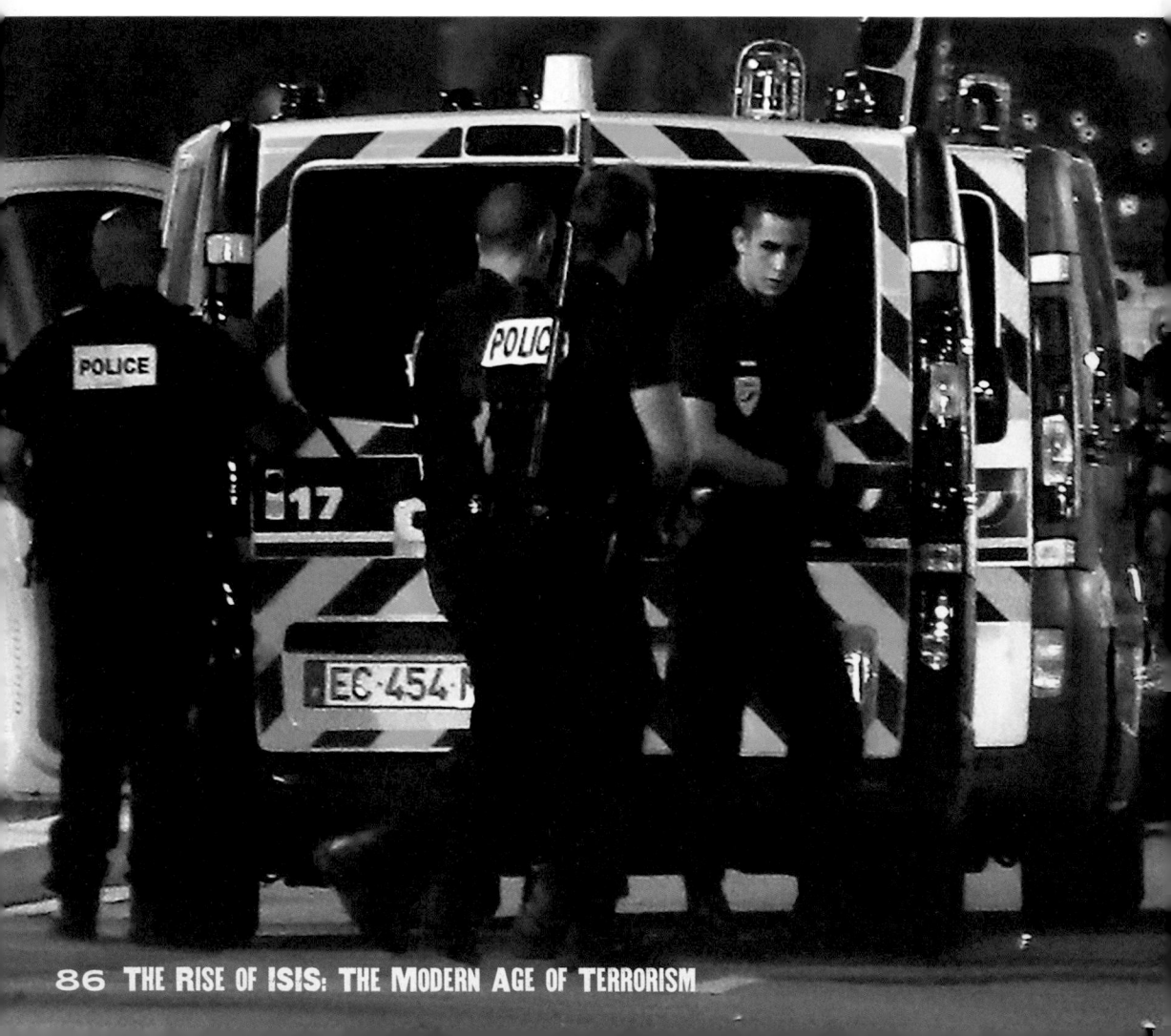

of Muslims of the Alpes-Maritimes said of the massacre,

> This is complicated in terms of mourning for the whole world; this is also a little complicated for the Muslim community which is afraid that acts of violence [will be directed at them]. We hope that this sends a global message that the barbarity touches the whole world and that the people here, the victims, are not those who commit the crimes in Syria and Iraq.[40,]

The Islamic State carries out these attacks to generate fear, resentment, and anger. Unfortunately, these negative feelings are not just directed specifically at the Islamic State. Many people around the world feel afraid of Muslims in general, even though nearly all followers of Islam are opposed to ISIS. This is all part of the Islamic State's plan: By spreading terror and hatred, it creates dividing lines between the people who could unify to fight back against it.

Terrorist incidents are designed to be devastating and cause as much damage as possible. This picture shows the aftermath of the attack in Nice, France.

Limiting the Growth of Terror

Worldwide fear of Muslims is reckless, prejudicial, and illogical. However, it is true that a small number of foreign Muslims are turning toward the Islamic State. It is nearly impossible to determine who is a deadly threat before they finally become one. Richard Walton, leader of the counterterrorism unit for the London Metropolitan Police during the 2012 Olympics, said,

> It's very easy retrospectively, with hindsight, to say that law enforcement, or government, should have known about someone's intent. But obviously there's a big difference between motivation—someone being radicalized—and then going out and actually acting on that. At any one time, in any country, there will be many hundreds, if not several thousand suspects, that fit this profile.[41]

Some countries are revoking the passports of suspected Muslim extremists. This prevents ISIS from growing stronger in one central geographic area. However, it also keeps people who sympathize with the Islamic State inside Western countries and worsens feelings of frustration and anger toward their native nations. In June 2016, a man named Larossi Abballa killed an off-duty French police officer and his wife. He posted a public video to Facebook immediately afterward saying, "I pledge allegiance to ... Abu Bakr al-Baghdadi ... I address this also to the French infidel authorities. This is the result of your work. You closed the door to my Hijrah. You closed the door toward the lands of the caliphate? Well, good then, we have opened the door of jihad onto your territory."[42] Abballa used the word Hijrah, which means "pilgrimage" in Arabic. Foreigners who want to travel to Syria and join ISIS often use this word to describe their attempts. Since he was unable to make that journey, however, he acted independently to destroy the lives he could while still at home.

Omar Mateen, the man who killed 49 people in a Florida nightclub, had a file that was just one of thousands kept by the U.S. intelligence services. France has one of the largest numbers of suspected Islamic State loyalists. Its list has 10,000 names on it and no ranking according to threat level. Each name has to be treated with the same degree of severity—but with 10,000 names, it is impossible to effectively investigate them. There is no way to put 10,000 French citizens on surveillance. Some French authorities have resigned themselves to the fact that this is a threat that will never go away.

Fighting ISIS from Denmark

Learning to live with this threat does not mean that the world should ignore it or assume it is fighting a losing battle. There are communities, such as one in Denmark, that have actively addressed the problem of young Muslims being drawn to the violence of the Islamic State—and successfully neutralized it.

In 2012, the police of the Danish town of Aarhus started to get calls about missing teenagers who lived in a Muslim immigrant neighborhood. Investigations revealed that the teenagers had traveled to Syria to join the Islamic State. Most of Europe has little tolerance—and with good reason—for anyone suspected of collaborating with ISIS. France has shut down mosques suspected of hiding potential jihadists, the United Kingdom calls those who travel to Syria and Iraq enemies of the state, and many countries revoke passports.

Police offers in Denmark, however, decided to take a different approach when dealing with possible extremist Muslims. They wanted to make it clear to all citizens who traveled to Syria that they would be welcome if they wanted to come back home to Europe. Moreover, if they wanted to come back, they would be given help and guidance on integrating back into society. This is now called the Aarhus model.

This approach was designed and implemented because the Danish officers thought that condemning these teenagers would only make them angrier and more dangerous. After all, they were only teenagers; their decision to leave was probably made hastily and emotionally. The officers knew that if they offered to help them instead of rejecting them, they could also keep an eye on them in case their situations did eventually escalate into something violent or dangerous.

Arie Kruglanski, a social psychologist at the University of Maryland, has written about using this approach:

The original response was to fight [extremism] through military and policing efforts, and they didn't fare too well. That kind of response that puts them as suspects and constrains them and promotes discrimination— that is only likely to [make] the problem [worse]. It's only likely to inflame the sense there's discrimination and motivate young people to act against society.[43]

If a young Muslim is attracted to the ideals of the Islamic State, it is often because they feel excluded from general society for being different. If their home countries and governments react to their feelings with suspicion and distrust, it could very well make the situation permanently worse. Kruglanski also said, "there are strong correlations between humiliation and the search for an extremist ideology."[44] Organizations such as the Islamic State prey on people who feel rejected by other communities.

From 2012 to July 2016, 34 people from Aarhus went to Syria. Six of them were killed, and ten are still in Syria. However, 18 came back to Denmark and showed up at the door to the police station. Hundreds of potential extremists have also gone to the police asking

Aarhus, Denmark, is attempting to prevent its Muslim youth from traveling to Syria and participating in the violence.

for help to integrate successfully into Danish society. Although this Danish town is a very small sample of a large-scale global problem, it does prove that positive reinforcement and messages of acceptance can make an impact on the lives of individual people—people who might have caused tragedy and death otherwise.

ISIS Predicting Its Own Destruction

In July 2016, public messages online communicated that Islamic State leaders were acknowledging that their fortunes were declining, and ISIS is currently losing territory instead of gaining it. Not only does this affect its

claim as an institution—if it claims to be a "state," ISIS needs land—but also limits its ability to raise money and train recruits.

Although this sounds like good news, the structure of the organization ensures that it will remain dangerous. An Islamic State operative said, "While we see our core structure in Iraq and Syria under attack, we have been able to expand and have shifted some of our command, media and wealth structure to different countries. We do have, every day, people reaching out and telling us they want to come to the caliphate, but we tell them to stay in their countries and rather wait to do something there."[45]

The Islamic State's earlier policy was to call its fighters to physically relocate to its territory. Now that its territory is shrinking and ISIS is recommending that its fighters do their duty from inside their home countries, it poses a large threat of more terrorist attacks being carried out in foreign countries.

In the first half of 2016, the geographic size of the Islamic State was reportedly reduced by 12 percent due to the efforts made by Iraqi government–controlled forces. Reports said that in some areas held by ISIS, Internet and television access is restricted to cut off the outside world. The State's weekly Arabic newsletter recently acknowledged the possibility that the entire territory could be lost. However, it insisted that the State itself would survive even if all the cities it occupied fell to its enemies.

ISIS officials compare the loss of territory to the situation in 2008 when the group was almost destroyed by the American troops and Sunni Arab tribes. The Islamic State has not admitted to any mistakes on their part that have led to their military disadvantage, but they do want to brace their followers for any possibilities yet to come. The task of anti-ISIS forces is to make sure that the apocalypse that Abu Bakr al-Baghdadi and his followers have been predicting never comes to pass.

Notes

Introduction:
From Islam to ISIS
1. Quoted in CNN Library, "ISIS Fast Facts," November 1, 2016. www.cnn.com/2014/08/08/world/isis-fast-facts/.

Chapter One:
Bin Laden, al-Zarqawi, and AQI
2. Quoted in "Ayman al-Zawahiri: Profile," CNN. www.cnn.com/CNN/Programs/people/shows/zawahiri/profile.html.
3. Quoted in Mary Ann Weaver, "The Short, Violent Life of Abu Musab al-Zarqawi," *The Atlantic*, July/August 2006. www.theatlantic.com/magazine/archive/2006/07/the-short-violent-life-of-abu-musab-al-zarqawi/304983/.
4. Quoted in Mary Ann Weaver, "The Short, Violent Life of Abu Musab al-Zarqawi."
5. Quoted in Michael Weiss and Hassan Hassan, *ISIS: Inside the Army of Terror.* New York, NY: Regan Arts, 2015, p. 10.

6. Quoted in Mary Ann Weaver, "The Short, Violent Life of Abu Musab al-Zarqawi."
7. Quoted in Mary Ann Weaver, "The Short, Violent Life of Abu Musab al-Zarqawi."
8. Quoted in William McCants, *The ISIS Apocalypse.* New York, NY: Picador, 2015, p.11.
9. Quoted in McCants, *The ISIS Apocalypse*, p.13.

Chapter Two:
Al-Masri and the Creation of the Islamic State
10. Quoted in McCants, *The ISIS Apocalypse*, p.19.

Chapter Three:
Abu Bakr al-Baghdadi
11. Quoted in William McCants, "Who Exactly is Abu Bakr al-Baghdadi, the Leader of ISIS?," *Newsweek*, September 15, 2015. www.newsweek.com/who-exactly-abu-bakr-al-baghdadi-leader-isis-368907.

12. Quoted in William McCants, "Who Exactly is Abu Bakr al-Baghdadi, the Leader of ISIS?"
13. Quoted in McCants, *The ISIS Apocalypse*, pp. 75–76.
14. Quoted in Graeme Wood, "What ISIS Really Wants," *The Atlantic*, March 2015. www.theatlantic.com/magazine/archive/2015/03/what-isis-really-wants/384980/.

Chapter Four:
Syria, Mosul, and the
Establishment of the Caliphate

15. Quoted in Joe Sterling, "Daraa: The Spark that Lit the Syrian Flame," CNN, March 1, 2012. www.cnn.com/2012/03/01/world/meast/syria-crisis-beginnings/.
16. Quoted in Profile: "Syria's al-Nusra Front," BBC, April 10, 2013. www.bbc.com/news/world-middle-east-18048033.
17. Quoted in McCants, *The ISIS Apocalypse*, p. 90.
18. Quoted in McCants, *The ISIS Apocalypse*, p. 98.
19. Quoted in Liz Sly and Ahmed Ramadan, "Insurgents Seize Iraqi City of Mosul as Security Forces Flee," *Washington Post*, June 10, 2014. www.washingtonpost.com/world/insurgents-seize-iraqi-city-of-mosul-as-troops-flee/2014/06/10/21061e87-8fcd-4ed3-bc94-0e309af0a674_story.html.
20. Quoted in Chelsea J. Carter and Hamdi Alkhshali, "Video Emerges of Purported Militant Leader in Mosul Preaching Holy War," CNN, July 5, 2014. www.cnn.com/2014/07/05/world/meast/iraq-crisis/.
21. Quoted in William McCants, "Who Exactly is Abu Bakr al-Baghdadi, the Leader of ISIS?"
22. Quoted in Graeme Wood, "What ISIS Really Wants."

Chapter Five:
The Caliphate and the
Coming Apocalypse

23. David Cook, *Contemporary Muslim Apocalyptic Literature*. Syracuse, NY: Syracuse University Press, 2005, p. 8.
24. Quoted in Graeme Wood, "What ISIS Really Wants."
25. Quoted in Rick Noack, "The ISIS Apocalypse Has Been Postponed but the Militants Might Still Believe in It," *Washington Post*, October 17, 2016. www.washingtonpost.com/news/worldviews/wp/2016/10/17/the-isis-apocalypse-has-been-postponed-but-the-militants-might-still-believe-in-it/?utm_term=.651bccd609c0.
26. Quoted in McCants, *The ISIS Apocalypse*, p. 104.
27. Quoted in Mariam Karouny, "Apocalyptic prophecies drive

both sides to Syrian battle for end of time," *Reuters*, April 1, 2014. www.reuters.com/article/us-syria-crisis-prophecy-insight-idUSBREA3013420140401.

28. Quoted in David D. Kirkpatrick, "New Freedoms in Tunisia Drive Support for ISIS," *New York Times*, October 21, 2014. www.nytimes.com/2014/10/22/world/africa/new-freedoms-in-tunisia-drive-support-for-isis.html.

29. Quoted in Graeme Wood, "What ISIS Really Wants."

30. Quoted in McCants, *The ISIS Apocalypse*, p. 124.

31. Quoted in McCants, *The ISIS Apocalypse*, p. 130.

Chapter Six:
The Impact of ISIS

32. Quoted in Weiss and Hassan, *ISIS: Inside the Army of Terror*, p. ix.

33. Quoted in Weiss and Hassan, *ISIS: Inside the Army of Terror*, p. xii.

34. Quoted in McCants, *The ISIS Apocalypse*, p. 140.

35. Quoted in Susannah Cullinane, Hamdi Alkhshali, and Mohammed Tawfeeq, "Tracking a Trail of Historical Obliteration: ISIS Trumpets Destruction of Nimrud," CNN, April 13, 2015. www.cnn.com/2015/03/09/world/iraq-isis-heritage/.

36. Quoted in Susannah Cullinane, Hamdi Alkhshali, and Mohammed Tawfeeq, "Tracking a Trail of Historical Obliteration: ISIS Trumpets Destruction of Nimrud."

37. Quoted in Susannah Cullinane, Hamdi Alkhshali, and Mohammed Tawfeeq, "Tracking a Trail of Historical Obliteration: ISIS Trumpets Destruction of Nimrud."

38. Quoted in Susannah Cullinane, Hamdi Alkhshali, and Mohammed Tawfeeq, "Tracking a Trail of Historical Obliteration: ISIS Trumpets Destruction of Nimrud."

39. Quoted in Anand Gopal, "The Hell After ISIS," *The Atlantic*, May 2016. www.theatlantic.com/magazine/archive/2016/05/the-hell-after-isis/476391/.

Epilogue:
ISIS Worldwide

40. Quoted in Alissa J. Rubin and Lilia Blaise, "A Third of Nice Truck Attack's Dead Were Muslim, Group Says," *New York Times*, July 19, 2016. www.nytimes.com/2016/07/20/world/europe/nice-truck-attack-victims-muslims.html.

41. Quoted in Rukmini Callimachi, "How Do You Stop a Future Terrorist When the Only Evidence Is a Thought?," *New York Times*, June 21, 2016. www.nytimes.com/2016/06/22/world/europe/france-orlando-isis-terrorism-investigation.html.

42. Quoted in Rukmini Callimachi, "How Do You Stop a Future

Terrorist When the Only Evidence Is a Thought?"

43. Quoted in Hanna Rosin, "How A Danish Town Helped Young Muslims Turn Away From ISIS," NPR, July 15, 2016. www.npr.org/sections/health-shots/2016/07/15/485900076/how-a-danish-town-helped-young-muslims-turn-away-from-isis?utm_source=facebook.com&utm_medium=social&utm_campaign=npr&utm_term=nprnews&utm_content=20160715.

44. Quoted in Hanna Rosin, "How A Danish Town Helped Young Muslims Turn Away From ISIS."

45. Quoted in Joby Warrick and Souad Mekhennet, "Inside ISIS: Quietly Preparing for the Loss of the 'Caliphate'," *Washington Post*, July 12, 2016. www.washingtonpost.com/world/national-security/inside-isis-quietly-preparing-for-the-loss-of-the-calipate/2016/07/12/9a1a8a02-454b-11e6-8856-f26de2537a9d_story.html.

For More Information

Books

Aslan, Reza. *No god but God: The Origins and Evolution of Islam*. New York, NY: Random House, 2005.
 An introduction to the religion of Islam for young readers, this book looks into its rituals and traditions.

McCants, William. *The ISIS Apocalypse: The History, Strategy, and Doomsday Vision of the Islamic State*. New York, NY: St. Martin's Press, 2015.
 McCants's book gives a detailed history of how ISIS was formed in a straightforward and easy-to-understand way.

National Geographic. *1001 Inventions and Awesome Facts from Muslim Civilization*. Washington, DC: National Geographic Children's Books, 2012.
 This short work describes the inventions made by Muslims in the early centuries that still influence modern life today.

Shuaib, Shurayh. *Introduction to Islamic Eschatology: Understanding Reality*. Seattle, WA: Amazon Digital Services, LLC, 2016.
 This e-book explains Islamic eschatology in the Koran, which means the part of Islam that deals with the apocalypse and the end of the world.

Yousafzai, Malala. *I Am Malala: The Girl Who Stood Up for Education and Was Shot by the Taliban*. London, UK: Orion Publishing Group Ltd., 2013.
 This book is the memoir of a Pakistani girl whose family was uprooted by terrorism and who was shot by a terrorist for speaking out.

Websites

A Brief History of ISIS
theweek.com/articles/589924/brief-history-isis
> This website is a recently written history of the Islamic State, with good information and tools for research.

ISIS: A Short History
www.theatlantic.com/international/archive/2014/08/isis-a-short-history/376030/
> This gives a brief overview of some of the basics of the founding and structure of ISIS.

The Secret History of ISIS
www.pbs.org/wgbh/frontline/film/the-secret-history-of-isis/
> This website has a link to a film featured on the PBS series *Frontline*, concerning who al-Zarqawi was and how he became famous.

Timeline: Rise and Spread of the Islamic State
www.wilsoncenter.org/article/timeline-rise-and-spread-the-islamic-state
> This timeline is a detailed list of many of the important dates and events surrounding ISIS and organizations like it.

You Can't Understand ISIS If You Don't Know the History of Wahhabism in Saudi Arabia
www.huffingtonpost.com/alastair-crooke/isis-wahhabism-saudi-arabia_b_5717157.html
> This website gives a history of Wahhabism in Saudi Arabia, explaining where some of the thought behind the Islamic State came from.

Index

Picture Credits

Cover Gokhan Sahin/Getty Images; p. 6 (top left) DOD via Getty Images; p. 6 (bottom left) AFP/Getty Images, p. 6 (background, bottom left) Frederic Legrand - COMEO/Shutterstock.com; pp. 6–7 (background, city) Orlok/Shutterstock.com; pp. 6–7 (background, man and child), 7 (background, bottom right) thomas koch/Shutterstock.com; p. 7 (top left) ASSOCIATED PRESS/AP Images; p. 7 (top right) Ali Mohammed/Anadolu Agency/Getty Images; p. 7 (bottom) SABAH ARAR/AFP/Getty Images; pp. 7 (background, top left), 41 railway fx/Shutterstock.com, p. 9 © iStockphoto.com/omersukrugoksu; p. 11 Steve Allen/The Image Bank/Getty Images; p. 12 Fine Art Images/Heritage Images/Getty Images; p. 17 Getty Images/Staff; p. 18 © iStockphoto.com/cosmonaut; p. 21 Maher Attar/Sygma via Getty Images; p. 23 Salah Malkawi/Getty Images; p. 25 Dan Howell/Shutterstock.com; p. 27 Chip HIRES/Gamma-Rapho via Getty Images; p. 29 Mario Tama/Getty Images; p. 31 © iStockphoto.com/oneinchpunch; p. 33 Patrick ROBERT/Corbis via Getty Images; pp. 34–35 MANDEL NGAN/AFP/Getty Images; p. 39 MARWAN IBRAHIM/AFP/Getty Images; p. 44 Al-Furqan Media/Anadolu Agency/Getty Images; p. 47 KHALIL MAZRAAWI/AFP/Getty Images; p. 49 Angela N Perryman/Shutterstock.com; pp. 50–51 DAVID FURST/AFP/Getty Images; p. 57 deepspace/Shutterstock.com; pp. 58–59 ART production/Shutterstock.com; p. 60 Jiri Flogel/Shutterstock.com; pp. 62–63 © iStockphoto.com/myhrcat; p. 68 frees/Shutterstock.com; p. 70 Handout/Alamy Stock Photo; p. 71 John Grummitt/Shutterstock.com; pp. 72–73 NurPhoto/NurPhoto via Getty Images; pp. 78–79 Joe Raedle/Getty Images; pp. 80–81 ChameleonsEye/Shutterstock.com; pp. 86–87 VALERY HACHE/AFP/Getty Images; p. 90 Anthon Jackson/Shutterstock.com.

About the Author

Caroline Kennon is a college librarian originally from Yonkers, New York. She got her bachelor's and master's degrees in English from St. Bonaventure University in Western New York, and her master's degree in Library Science from the University at Buffalo. She is an avid reader, a novice cyclist, and a cheese addict. She currently lives in South Buffalo, New York—the winters really are not that bad.